SPECTRUM

Grade 4

TEXAS
Test Prep

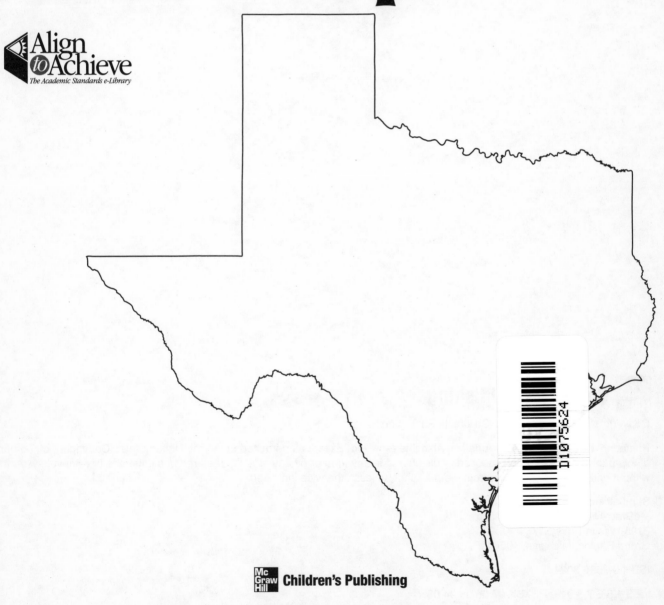

McGraw Hill **Children's Publishing**

Children's Publishing

Send all inquiries to:
McGraw-Hill Children's Publishing
3195 Wilson Drive NW
Grand Rapids, Michigan 49544

ISBN 0-7696-3024-3

2 3 4 5 6 7 8 9 10 PHXBK 07 06 05 04 03

The McGraw-Hill Companies

Table of Contents

Mathematics

What's Inside?

This workbook is designed to help you and your fourth-grader understand what he or she will be expected to know on the Texas fourth-grade state tests. The testing program, called the Texas Assessment of Knowledge and Skills (TAKS), measures student learning in different subject areas,

Practice Pages

The workbook is divided into a Language Arts section and Mathematics section. Each section has practice activities that have questions similar to those that will appear on the state tests. Students should use a pencil to fill in the correct answers and to complete any writing on these activities.

Texas Content Standards

Before each practice section is a list of the state standards covered by that section. The shaded "What it means" sections will help to explain any information in the standards that might be unfamiliar.

Mini-Tests and Final Tests

Practice activities are grouped by state standard. When each group is completed the student can move on to a Mini-Test that covers the material presented on those practice activities. After an entire set of standards and accompanying activities are completed, the student should take the Final Tests, which incorporate materials from all the practice activities in that section.

Final Test Answer Sheet

The Final Tests have a separate answer sheet that mimics the style of the answer sheet the students will use on the state tests. The answer sheet appears at the end of each Final Test.

How Am I Doing?

The How Am I Doing? pages are designed to help students identify areas where they are proficient and areas where they still need more practice. Students can keep track of each of their Mini-Test scores on these pages.

Answer Key

Answers to all the practice activities, mini-tests, and final tests are listed by page number and appear at the end of the book.

What kinds of information does my child have to know to pass the test?

The Texas Education Agency provides a list of the knowledge and skills that students are expected to master at each grade level. The practice activities in this workbook provide students with practice in each of these areas.

Are there special strategies or tips that will help my child do well?

The workbook provides sample questions that have content similar to that on the state tests. Test-taking tips are offered throughout the book.

How do I know what areas my child needs help in?

A special How Am I Doing? section will help you and your fourth-grader evaluate progress. It will pinpoint areas where more work is needed as well as areas where your student excels.

TAKS Content Standards

The reading section of the state test measures knowledge in four different areas.

Reading

1) Objective 1: Basic understanding of written texts

2) Objective 2: Applying knowledge of literary elements to understand written texts

3) Objective 3: Using a variety of strategies to analyze written texts

4) Objective 4: Applying critical-thinking skills to analyze written texts

Writing

1) Objective 1: Producing an effective composition for a specific purpose

2) Objective 2: Producing a piece of writing that demonstrates a command of the conventions of spelling, capitalization, punctuation, grammar, usage, and sentence structure

3) Objective 3: Recognizing appropriate organization of ideas in written text

4) Objective 4: Recognizing correct and effective sentence construction in written text

5) Objective 5: Recognizing standard usage and appropriate word choice in written text

6) Objective 6: Proofreading for correct punctuation, capitalization, and spelling in written text

Reading and Writing Table of Contents

TAKS Reading—Objective 1

The student will demonstrate a basic understanding of culturally diverse written texts.

(4.9) Reading/vocabulary development

The student acquires an extensive vocabulary through reading and systematic word study. The student is expected to

(B) draw on experiences to bring meanings to words in context such as interpreting figurative language and multiple-meaning words (4–5); and *(See pages 8–9.)*

What it means:
- Figurative language is language used for descriptive effect. It describes or implies meaning, rather than directly stating it. Examples of figurative language include:

  similes - using *like* or *as* to compare things that may seem unlike each other. Example: Her smile was as dazzling as the sun.

  metaphors - comparing unlike things but without using *like* or *as*. Example: His body was a well-oiled machine.

  hyperbole - using exaggeration to convey strong emotion, express humor, or emphasize a point. Example: I felt like we walked a million miles!

  personification - assigning human qualities, feelings, or actions to an animal, an object, or an idea. Example: The mother bear cried for her cub.
- Multiple-meaning words are spelled the same but have different meanings. Example: bill can mean the "beak of a bird" or "a monthly expense."

(D) determine meanings of derivatives by applying knowledge of the meanings of root words such as like, pay, or happy and affixes such as *dis-, pre-,* and *un-* (4–8). *(See page 10.)*

(4.10) Reading/comprehension

The student comprehends selections using a variety of strategies. The student is expected to

(F) determine a text's main (or major) ideas and how those ideas are supported with details (4–8); and *(See page 11.)*

(G) paraphrase and summarize text to recall, inform, or organize ideas (4–8). *(See page 12.)*

Reading/Vocabulary Development

Objective 1

Expectation: draw on experiences to bring meanings to words in context such as interpreting figurative language and multiple-meaning words

---

DIRECTIONS: Read the passage and then match each idiom with its meaning.

Food for Thought

A waiter was taking a break. He said to a brand new employee, "You just have to be the one <u>to break the ice</u> with the chef. Sometimes it seems like he has <u>a chip on his shoulder</u>, but he's okay. This is a busy place. You've jumped <u>out of the frying pan and into the fire</u>, let me tell you. I hope you don't have any <u>pie-in-the-sky</u> ideas about taking things easy here. Some days, I feel like I'm <u>going bananas</u>. It might not be your <u>cup of tea</u>. I think we've got <u>the cream of the crop</u> here; everybody does a great job. It's hard sometimes not to <u>fly off the handle</u> when things are so hectic, though. I think you'll do all right if you don't mind hard work.

1. _____ to break the ice

2. _____ a chip on his shoulder

3. _____ out of the frying pan and into the fire

4. _____ pie-in-the-sky

5. _____ going bananas

6. _____ cup of tea

7. _____ the cream of the crop

8. _____ fly off the handle

A. unrealistic

B. something one enjoys

C. the best available

D. to make a start

E. to lose one's temper

F. seemingly angry or resentful

G. go crazy

H. from a bad situation to a worse one

Reading/Vocabulary Development

Objective 1

Expectation: draw on experiences to bring meanings to words in context such as interpreting figurative language and multiple-meaning words

---

DIRECTIONS: Choose the word that correctly completes both sentences.

9. Someone bought the _____ on the corner.

   A new house costs a _____ of money.

   - (A) bunch
   - (B) lot
   - (C) house
   - (D) property

10. Inez bought a _____ of soda.

    The doctor said it was a difficult _____.

    - (F) case
    - (G) carton
    - (H) disease
    - (J) situation

11. The _____ is flat.

    The runner began to _____.

    - (A) turn
    - (B) balloon
    - (C) lose
    - (D) tire

12. What _____ does Carl work?

    Help me _____ the box to that side.

    - (F) shift
    - (G) time
    - (H) move
    - (J) job

DIRECTIONS: Read the paragraph. Find the word below the paragraph that fits best in each numbered blank.

It takes a great deal of __13__ to become a champion in any sport. Many hours of practice are __14__, and you must often __15__ other aspects of your life.

13.
    - (A) inflammation
    - (B) dedication
    - (C) restriction
    - (D) location

14.
    - (F) required
    - (G) deflected
    - (H) extracted
    - (J) expanded

15.
    - (A) include
    - (B) neglect
    - (C) locate
    - (D) construct

STOP

Reading/Vocabulary Development

Objective
1

Expectation: determine meanings of derivatives by applying knowledge of the meanings of root words such as like, pay, or happy and affixes such as dis-, pre-, and un-

PREFIX BANK

Prefix	Meaning
anti-	against
be-	cause to be
co-	with or together
dis-	not or without
pre-	before
pro-	in place of
re-	again
un-	not

 Clue   A prefix is a word part that when added to a root word changes the word's meaning.

DIRECTIONS: Choose a prefix from the Prefix Bank and add it to the root word to make a new word. Then, use the new word in a sentence.

1. _____ + *view* = "to see before"

_____

_____

2. _____ + *happy* = "not happy"

_____

_____

3. _____ + *little* = "to cause to feel small"

_____

_____

4. _____ + *workers* = "people one works with"

_____

_____

5. _____ + *trust* = "without trust"

_____

_____

6. _____ + *play* = "to play again."

_____

_____

STOP

Reading/Comprehension

**Objective
1**

Expectation: determine a text's main (or major) ideas and how those ideas are supported with details

---

DIRECTIONS: Read the paragraph, then answer the questions.

Ellis Island

Thousands of immigrants arrived each day at Ellis Island in New York. This was one of the reception centers set up by the United States government. The immigrants arrived with high hopes. Many had a great deal to offer the United States. However, not all those who came through Ellis Island were allowed to stay in this country.

Immigrants had forms to fill out, questions to answer, and medical exams to face. They waited for many hours in the Great Hall to hear their names called. Many had spent months in poor conditions on ships to come to the United States to make a better life. They had spent their savings to make the trip. Even after this, some were turned away.

1. What is the main idea of paragraph 1?

- (A) Thousands of immigrants arrived each day at Ellis Island.
- (B) Many immigrants were not allowed to stay in the United States.
- (C) Immigrants to the United States arrived at Ellis Island in New York.
- (D) Many immigrants arrived in the United States at Ellis Island, but not all were allowed to stay.

2. What is the main idea of paragraph 2?

- (F) Many immigrants had to go through a lot to get into the United States, and some did not make it.
- (G) Immigrants had to stand in long lines.
- (H) Many immigrants were poor.
- (J) Immigrants stood in the Great Hall waiting for their names to be called.

STOP

Reading/Comprehension

Objective
1

Expectation: paraphrase and summarize text to recall, inform, or organize ideas

---

Breakfast of Winners

"Why Crunchy Munchy Bunches of Bananas and Bran Flakes Is My Favorite Cereal" Contest

Dear Cereal Maker,

    I try to eat your delicious cereal every day. It is my first choice for breakfast (except for cold pepperoni pizza—but Mom says I can only eat that on my birthday). Why do I like your cereal so much? First of all, Mom always says that I act like a monkey when I climb all over the furniture, and we all know that monkeys love bananas. Second, my big brother constantly tells me not to act so flaky! And your cereal has lots of big flakes. Anyway, I guess liking your cereal is just in my genes!

Your friend,

Horace

DIRECTIONS: Underline one sentence from **Group 1** and one sentence from **Group 2** to form a brief summary of the letter above.

Group 1

A A child has entered a contest to determine which contestant eats the most of a particular type of cereal.

B A child has entered a contest to determine which person has the best reasons for eating a particular brand of cereal.

Group 2

A He feels that his behaving like a monkey and acting a bit flaky should make him the winner.

B He feels that Crunchy Munchy Bunches of Bananas and Bran Flakes has the best combination of fruit and bran flakes.

Objective

1

For pages 8–12

Mini-Test

DIRECTIONS: Find the sentence in which the underlined word is used in the same way.

1. **The field is planted with corn.**
   - (A) The field of technology is always changing.
   - (B) We can see deer in the field by our house.
   - (C) Her field is nursing.
   - (D) Our field trip is next Thursday.

2. **The general idea was to weave a basket.**
   - (F) She is a general in the army.
   - (G) The soldiers followed their general into battle.
   - (H) I think that the general had the best idea.
   - (J) No general study of history can cover everything.

DIRECTIONS: Choose the answer that means the same as the underlined word.

3. **Fearless dog**
   - (A) careless
   - (B) energetic
   - (C) unafraid
   - (D) sincere

4. **Dishonest advertisement**
   - (F) trustworthy
   - (G) imaginary
   - (H) true
   - (J) false

DIRECTIONS: Read the passage, then answer the questions.

A Microscope

Have you ever looked into a microscope? A microscope is an instrument that helps us see very small things by magnifying them. Scientists and doctors can use microscopes to study parts of the body, such as blood and skin cells. They can also study germs, tiny plants, and tiny animals.

5. **In this passage, what does the word *instrument* mean?**
   - (A) a tool
   - (B) a drum
   - (C) an office
   - (D) a paper

6. **In this passage, what does the word *magnifying* mean?**
   - (F) making them smaller
   - (G) making them larger
   - (H) making them red
   - (J) making them disappear

7. **Which of these best summarizes the passage?**
   - (A) A microscope helps us see small things by magnifying them.
   - (B) A microscope helps us see blood cells.
   - (C) A microscope is an instrument.
   - (D) A microscope helps doctors and scientists.

TAKS Reading—Objective 2

The student will apply knowledge of literary elements to understand culturally diverse written texts.

(4.12) Reading/text structures/literary concepts

The student analyzes the characteristics of various types of texts (genres). The student is expected to

(H) analyze characters, including their traits, motivations, conflicts, points of view, relationships, and changes they undergo (4–8); and (*See pages 15–16.*)

(I) recognize and analyze story plot, setting, and problem resolution (4–8). (*See pages 17–18.*)

Name _____ Date _____

Reading/Text Structures/Literary Concepts

Objective 2

Expectation: *analyze characters, including their traits, motivations, conflicts, points of view, relationships, and changes they undergo*

DIRECTIONS: Read the passage and answer the questions on page 16.

Volcano Adventure

"OK," said Sara. "Let's take this experiment one step at a time. First, we have to build a sand volcano with this film can inside of it."

"Let's make it really tall!" said Abdul. "I'll help!"

"Are you sure this won't blow up?" asked Tim, looking worried. "I've read that science labs blow up all the time."

Valerie yawned. "Oh, come on, Tim! Don't be silly." She studied her nails while the other three students built the sand volcano.

"Good," said Sara. "Now we mix the red food coloring into this vinegar. The volcano won't be red, but the 'lava' will."

"That's great! This is going to be the coolest thing!" said Abdul. "I got to see a real volcano in Hawaii." He bent over to watch Sara mixing the liquids together.

"Really, Abdul?" asked Tim. "Weren't you afraid it would blow up while you were standing there?"

"No," said Abdul. "It wasn't scary."

"Abdul, would you please hold this funnel?" asked Sara. "Valerie, will you put the baking soda in the volcano?"

"Oh, how thrilling," said Valerie, rolling her eyes. "I think I'll just stand here and watch the rest of you scientists."

"Here, Tim, you can do it," said Sara. "Just fill it halfway."

"This isn't going to blow up in my face, is it?" Tim looked nervous as he spooned the powder into the volcano. Sara read the instruction sheet. "No, there's no reaction until we pour the vinegar on it," she said.

Tim jumped back. "Don't pour yet!"

"The film can is like the underground chamber of the volcano," said Abdul. "The red lava is really melted rock that's forced to the surface by hot gases. That's why the lava is red . . . it's red hot. After it cools down, it turns back into a solid again. Then it's called pumice."

Valerie yawned and looked out the window. Sara said, "Is everyone ready? I'm going to pour in the vinegar now."

Tim moved back against the bookshelves. Abdul leaned forward to watch. He grinned as the soda "erupted" over the top of the volcano. "Wow! It looks like the real thing!" he said. "Let's do it again!"

Reading/Text Structures/Literary Concepts

Objective
2

Expectation: analyze characters, including their traits, motivations, conflicts, points of view, relationships, and changes they undergo

---

DIRECTIONS: Answer the following questions based on your reading of the passage.

Each student went home and told his or her parents about the science lab. Write the name of each character above each description.

1. _____

   "We did an experiment where a volcano actually erupted right in class! But it was OK. Nobody was hurt."

2. _____

   "We did an experiment and built a volcano model. It was very important that we followed the instructions to make it work."

3. _____

   "We built a model of a volcano that worked like the real thing! We actually made a mixture that was red like lava. Then we made the volcano erupt! It was so great, I wanted to do it again!"

4. _____

   "We did some kind of science thing. I don't really remember."

5. **Which character seems most excited?**

   _____

6. **Which character seems least interested?**

   _____

7. **Which character seems fearful?**

   _____

8. **Which character seems calm?**

   _____

9. **Which character seems the most organized?**

   _____

10. **Which character seems bored by school?**

    _____

Reading/Text Structures/Literary Concepts

Objective 2

Expectation: *recognize and analyze story plot, setting, and problem resolution*

DIRECTIONS: Read the passage and answer the questions on page 18.

Minnie the Mole

Minnie the Mole and her five children live in a cozy burrow under Mr. Smith's garden. Minnie works hard gathering insects and worms, her five children's favorite treats. It is not an easy job since moles eat their own weight in food each day.

Mr. Smith did not like the raised roofs of Minnie's tunnels in his garden. One hot summer day, as Minnie was digging through the bean patch with her sharp claws, she heard a new sound. Although she has no external ears, Minnie can hear very well. Mr. Smith was pounding a trap into position at the front entrance to her burrow.

Minnie hurried home and gathered her children around her. "We are in danger! We must move quickly. Get in line and follow me," demanded Minnie. The little moles with their short, stocky bodies and long snouts did as their mother told them.

Minnie started digging a tunnel in the soft soil as fast as she could. "We're going to Uncle Marty Mole's burrow. We'll be safer there," Minnie said. She and the children worked tirelessly for two hours. They were far from Mr. Smith's garden now. Tired, but safe, the little group rested in the comfort of Uncle Marty's living room.

"You were busy as beavers today," said Uncle Marty.

"I'd say we were more like a 'mole machine'!" laughed Minnie.

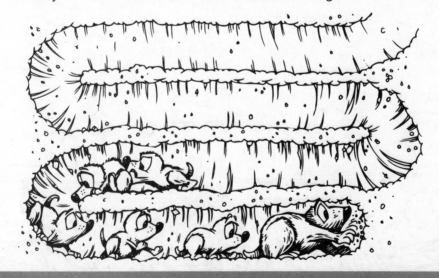

GO ⟹

Reading/Text Structures/Literary Concepts

Objective
2

Expectation: *recognize and analyze story plot, setting, and problem resolution*

DIRECTIONS: Answer the questions about the story.

1. **The main character is** _____ .

2. **The first setting for the story is** _____ .

3. **Mr. Smith didn't like having moles in his garden because** _____ .

4. **Minnie's problem was that Mr. Smith** _____ .

5. **First, Minnie told her children to** _____ .

6. **They dug for** _____ .

7. **The problem was solved when** _____ .

8. **Uncle Marty said Minnie and her children had worked like** _____ .

9. **Minnie said they had worked more like a** _____ .

STOP

Objective

2

Mini-Test

DIRECTIONS: Read the story, then answer the questions.

> Cassie's mom has errands to run, so Cassie agrees to stay home to babysit for her little brother, who is asleep. Her mom also leaves Cassie a list of chores to do while she is gone. Cassie will be able to go to the mall with her friends when her chores are finished and her mom gets back. As soon as Cassie's mom leaves, Cassie starts calling her friends on the phone. She talks to Kim for 20 minutes and to Beth for 15 minutes. She is supposed to call Maria when she finishes talking to Jackie.
>
> After talking on the phone, Cassie decides to do her nails while she watches a movie on TV. After the movie, Cassie listens to the radio and reads a magazine. Before Cassie realizes it, three and a half hours have passed and her mom is back home. Her mom walks in and finds the kitchen still a mess, crumbs all over the carpet, dusty furniture, and Cassie's little brother screaming in his room.

1. **What is the setting for this story?**
   - (A) the mall
   - (B) Cassie's house
   - (C) Jackie's house
   - (D) the kitchen

2. **What do we know about the main character?**
   - (F) she has errands to run
   - (G) she has chores to do
   - (H) he is asleep
   - (J) he is screaming in his room

3. **What is the plot of this story?**
   - (A) Cassie must do her chores if she wants to go to the mall. But, she wastes the time instead.
   - (B) Cassie's mother has errands to run. She leaves Cassie in charge of the house.
   - (C) Cassie's brother is asleep in his room. He wakes up screaming.
   - (D) Cassie is grounded.

4. **Which of the following is a chore Cassie probably wasn't supposed to do?**
   - (F) dust
   - (G) listen for her brother
   - (H) do her nails
   - (J) clean the kitchen

5. **What do you think the resolution to this problem will be?**
   - (A) Cassie's little brother will have to do all the chores.
   - (B) Cassie will be punished and will not go to the mall.
   - (C) Cassie's mom will drive her to the mall.
   - (D) Cassie, her mom, and her brother will go to a movie.

TAKS Reading—Objective 3

The student will use a variety of strategies to analyze culturally diverse written texts.

(4.10) Reading/comprehension
The student comprehends selections using a variety of strategies.
The student is expected to

(E) use the text's structure or progression of ideas such as cause and effect or chronology to locate and recall information (4–8); (*See page 21.*)

(I) find similarities and differences across texts such as in treatment, scope, or organization (4–8); and (*See page 22.*)

(L) represent text information in different ways such as in outline, timeline, or graphic organizer (4–8). (*See page 23.*)

(4.12) Reading/text structures/literary concepts
The student analyzes the characteristics of various types of texts (genres).
The student is expected to

(A) judge the internal consistency or logic of stories and texts such as "Would this character do this?"; "Does this make sense here?" (4–5); (*See page 24.*)

(C) identify the purposes of different types of texts such as to inform, influence, express, or entertain (4–8); (*See page 25.*)

(E) compare communication in different forms such as [contrasting a dramatic performance with a print version of the same story or] comparing story variants ((2–8); and (*See page 26.*)

(J) describe how the author's perspective or point of view affects the text (4–8). (*See pages 27–28.*)

What it means:
- Genre is a type, or category, of literature. Some examples of genre include fiction, biographies, poetry, and fables. Each genre is characterized by various differences in form. For example, a fable differs from the broader category of fiction in that it has a moral or character lesson.

Reading/Comprehension

Objective 3

Expectation: use the text's structure or progression of ideas such as cause and effect or chronology to locate and recall information

---

Clouds

Do you like to watch clouds float by? You may have noticed that there are many different shapes of clouds. Clouds are named for the way they look. Cirrus clouds are thin and high in the sky. Stratus clouds are low and thick. Cumulus clouds are white and puffy.

Do you know how clouds are formed? The air holds water that the warm sun has pulled, or evaporated, from Earth. When this water cools in the air, it forms clouds. When a cloud forms low along the ground, it is called fog. Clouds hold water until they become full. Warm clouds that are full of water produce rain; cold clouds that are full of water produce snow. When water falls to Earth as either rain or snow, it is called *precipitation.*

DIRECTIONS: Answer the questions about the passage.

1. **What is the effect of water cooling in the air?**
   - (A) Evaporation occurs.
   - (B) The sun warms Earth.
   - (C) Fog forms.
   - (D) Clouds form.

2. **Which sentence explains what causes fog?**
   - (F) A cloud forms low to the ground.
   - (G) A cloud is white and puffy.
   - (H) A cloud is thin and high in the sky.
   - (J) A cloud is full.

3. **One effect of evaporation is _____ .**
   - (A) rain creates moisture in the soil
   - (B) the air holds water
   - (C) clouds float through the sky
   - (D) the sun pulls clouds higher

4. **Write three short sentences that explain how clouds are formed.**

   _____

   _____

   _____

   _____

   _____

   _____

   _____

   _____

   _____

   _____

   _____

   _____

Reading/Comprehension

Objective 3

Expectation: *find similarities and differences across texts such as in treatment, scope, or organization*

Maggie and Isabel went to the park on Saturday. They both headed for the slides. But, they couldn't decide who should go first. Isabel said she should because she was older. Maggie said she should go first because Isabel always got to. Just then, their mother came over and said, "Why don't you each get on one slide and start down at the same time?"

And that's just what they did.

Joel's hockey team had been playing well all season, and this was their chance to win the tournament. He was their best player.

He glanced around at his teammates. "Guys," he said. "Let's skate really hard and show them how great we are!"

The team cheered and started to walk out to the ice. Joel turned around to grab his helmet, but it wasn't there. He looked under the benches and in the lockers, but his helmet wasn't anywhere. He sat down and felt his throat get tight. If he didn't have a helmet, he couldn't play.

Just then there was a knock on the door. Joel's mom peeked her head around the locker room door. "Thank goodness," she said. "I got here just in time with your helmet."

DIRECTIONS: Read both stories, then fill in the blank with the correct answer from the parentheses.

1. Both of the stories are _____ .

   (fiction / non-fiction)

2. Both stories are about _____ that gets solved.

   (an argument / a problem)

3. The person who solves the problem in both stories is _____ .

   (the coach / the mother)

4. If both of these stories appeared together in a book of similar stories, a good title for the book would be _____ .

   (*Sports Bloopers* / *Mom to the Rescue*)

Name _____ Date _____

Reading/Comprehension

Objective 3

Expectation: represent text information in different ways such as in outline, timeline, or graphic organizer

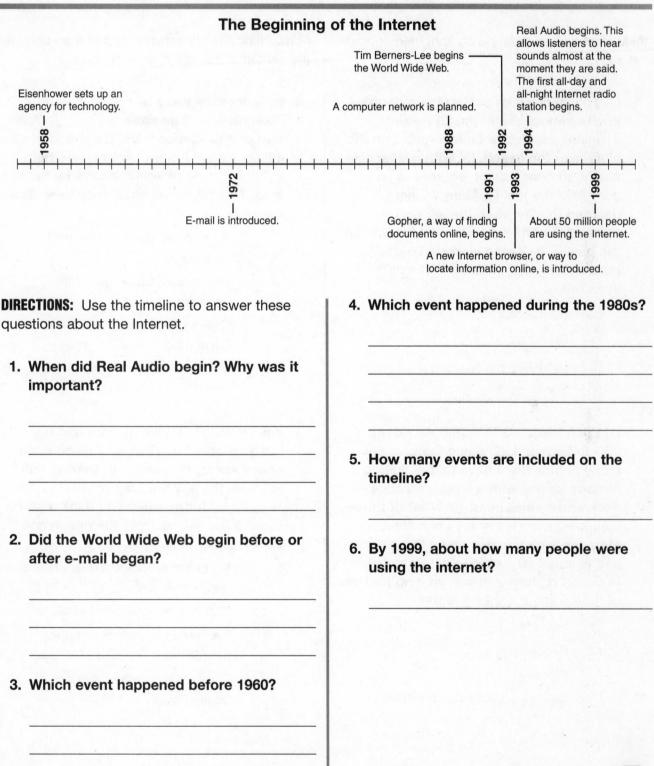

The Beginning of the Internet

Eisenhower sets up an agency for technology.
1958

1972
E-mail is introduced.

Tim Berners-Lee begins the World Wide Web.

A computer network is planned.
1988

Real Audio begins. This allows listeners to hear sounds almost at the moment they are said. The first all-day and all-night Internet radio station begins.
1992
1994

1991
Gopher, a way of finding documents online, begins.

1993
A new Internet browser, or way to locate information online, is introduced.

1999
About 50 million people are using the Internet.

DIRECTIONS: Use the timeline to answer these questions about the Internet.

1. When did Real Audio begin? Why was it important?

_____
_____
_____

2. Did the World Wide Web begin before or after e-mail began?

_____
_____

3. Which event happened before 1960?

_____
_____
_____

4. Which event happened during the 1980s?

_____
_____
_____
_____

5. How many events are included on the timeline?

_____

6. By 1999, about how many people were using the internet?

_____

STOP

Name _____ Date _____

Reading/Text Structures/Literary Concepts

Objective 3

Expectation: judge the internal consistency or logic of stories and texts such as "Would this character do this?"; "Does this make sense here?"

DIRECTIONS: Read each paragraph, then choose the sentence that does not belong.

1. (1) The sleepy little fishing town doubled in size almost overnight. (2) Harriet Johnson decided to build a resort on the cliffs near the beach. (3) With her fortune, she hired hundreds of workers to complete the job. (4) Many of them decided to stay when the job was finished. (5) The workers lived in tents on the beach. (6) These workers helped build the logging industry that exists even today.

   Ⓐ Sentence 2
   Ⓑ Sentence 3
   Ⓒ Sentence 4
   Ⓓ Sentence 5

2. (1) Loch Ness is a long and very deep lake in Scotland. (2) Since the year 565, many people there have told of seeing a strange animal with a long, snakelike neck and a small head. (3) Most of those who have seen it say the Loch Ness Monster is dark, has a hump like a camel, and is about 50 feet long. (4) Camels live in desert regions and can go long periods of time without drinking water.

   Ⓕ Sentence 1
   Ⓖ Sentence 2
   Ⓗ Sentence 3
   Ⓙ Sentence 4

DIRECTIONS: Read each paragraph, then choose the sentence that fits best in the blank.

3. In Tennessee there is a large, beautiful lake inside a giant cave. _____ Years ago people named it the "Lost Sea." In the 1800s, Native Americans and Southern soldiers would hide in the cave by the lake. This cave was once even used as a dance hall.

   Ⓐ Tennessee also has beautiful mountains.
   Ⓑ Lakes are usually filled with freshwater.
   Ⓒ Caves can contain stalactites or stalagmites.
   Ⓓ It is the world's largest underground lake.

4. You've heard of "raining cats and dogs," but how about fish? In an English town called Appin, thousands of herring fish fell from the sky one day in 1817. _____ Today scientists think a storm sucked the fish up from the ocean and dumped them inland.

   Ⓕ No one then could explain how this happened.
   Ⓖ Fish are usually found in water.
   Ⓗ Herring are a type of fish that people eat.
   Ⓙ There weren't many modern conveniences in 1817.

STOP

24

Name _____ Date _____

Reading/Text Structures/Literary Concepts

Objective
3

Expectation: *identify the purposes of different types of texts such as to inform, influence, express, or entertain*

The Abominable Snowman

The abominable snowman is a creature that may live on the highest mountain in the world, Mount Everest. Some people believe that it is just a bear or a gorilla. But it might also be an amazing creature.

The abominable snowman is also called the Yeti. It is thought to be a huge, hairy animal with a body like an ape and a head much like a human. Some people say that when the Yeti comes down from the mountain, it will attack the people and animals in the villages. But there are many more stories of the Yeti rescuing hikers lost in the snowy mountains.

There have been many reports of giant footprints in the snow. One group of explorers even photographed these footprints. The evidence is not clear whether the Yeti is real or not, but explorers should definitely try to learn more about this creature.

---

1. **The author's purpose for writing this passage is most likely _____ .**

   (A) to convince readers the abominable snowman is not real

   (B) to tell readers what it is like to hike on Mount Everest

   (C) to warn of the dangers of living in the snowy mountains

   (D) to encourage further study of the abominable snowman

2. **Which of the following is the author most likely to believe?**

   (F) Yeti is a real creature who is friendly.

   (G) Yeti is just a bear.

   (H) Yeti is just a gorilla.

   (J) Yeti is a real creature who is dangerous.

3. **Which words or phrases from the story showed you how the author felt about the Yeti?**

   _____

   _____

   _____

   _____

   _____

   _____

STOP

Reading/Text Structures/Literary Concepts

Objective 3

Expectation: *compare communication in different forms such as [contrasting a dramatic performance with a print version of the same story or] comparing story variants*

The Goldilocks Report

At 5:05 P.M., we were called to the home of a Mr. and Mrs. Bear. They had been out for the day. Upon returning, they found the lock on their door had been broken. Officer Paws and I went into the house. We found that food had been stolen and a chair had been broken. Paws searched the backyard while I went upstairs. I found a person asleep in a small bed. The subject is a female human with curly blonde hair. She was unknown to the Bear family. The human claimed her name was Goldilocks. She could not prove that fact. She will be questioned at the police station.

Officer Grizzly

DIRECTIONS: Answer the questions about the passage.

1. This is another view of the fairy tale _____ .

- (A) Goldilocks and Three Bears
- (B) Jack and the Beanstalk
- (C) Little Miss Muffet
- (D) Officer Grizzly and the Report

2. Which character tells the story "The Goldilocks Report"?

- (F) Goldilocks
- (G) Baby Bear
- (H) Papa Bear
- (J) Officer Grizzly

3. How is the ending of "The Goldilocks Report" different from the traditional fairy tale?

_____
_____
_____
_____
_____
_____
_____
_____
_____
_____

Reading/Text Structures/Literary Concepts

Objective 3

Expectation: *describe how the author's perspective or point of view affects the text*

DIRECTIONS: Read the passage and answer the questions on page 28.

A bicycle of the future may look very different from the one you ride now. One day you may be riding around on a recumbent bicycle—or even a tricycle!

On a recumbent cycle, the rider sits in a reclining position, in a comfortable, slung fabric seat, similar to a hammock. This position, with the legs extended forward, lets the cyclist use the greater strength in the upper legs to pedal.

Racers like these cycles because the streamlined position allows the rider to attain greater speeds. On an ordinary upright bicycle, air pushes against the rider's body to create wind resistance, which slows the rider down. To go faster, the rider puts his or her head down and straightens into as much of a horizontal position as possible. The recumbent cycle is more streamlined than an ordinary bicycle. The rider's reclined body position lowers wind resistance, and the cyclist goes faster.

Some people like three-wheeled recumbent cycles because they are steadier and safer than two-wheeled bicycles. That's important when a parent is transporting a small child on the back. Three-wheeled recumbent cycles can also carry heavy loads without falling over as easily as regular cycles.

Most recumbent cycles are lightweight, ride smoothly, and use standard parts. Many cyclists and bicycle designers believe that recumbent cycles will someday replace today's upright bicycles in popular use. They may look strange now, but what may seem strange today may not seem so strange tomorrow.

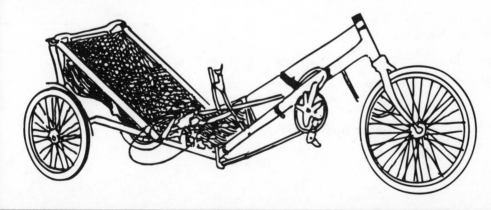

GO

Reading/Text Structures/
Literary Concepts

Objective
3

Expectation: *describe how the author's perspective or point of view affects the text*

1. **Find the best ending to the sentence. The author's purpose for writing this passage is to _____ .**

   (A) protect small children from bicycle accidents

   (B) alarm the reader about the dangers of bike riding

   (C) make the reader laugh

   (D) inform the reader about an unusual bicycle

2. **Which sentence tells the author's opinion?**

   (F) Change can be hard.

   (G) How we do things today may not be the way we do them in the future.

   (H) Small children can get hurt on bicycles.

   (J) Bicycle designers don't like three-wheelers.

3. **What title do you think the author would give to this passage?**

   (A) Slow but Popular

   (B) Bicycle of the Future

   (C) The History of Bicycles

   (D) Two Wheels are Better than Three

4. **Does the author think people will start riding recumbent cycles more in the future? Support your answer with clues from the passage.**

   _____

   _____

   _____

   _____

   _____

   _____

   _____

   _____

   _____

   _____

   _____

   _____

   _____

Objective

3

Mini-Test

DIRECTIONS: Read the story, then answer the questions.

Waterland

"Hurray!" cried Meghan. "Today is the day we're going to Waterland!" It was a hot July day, and Meghan's mom was taking her to cool off on the water slides. Meghan's new friend, Jake, was going, too.

Just then, Meghan's mom came out of her bedroom. She did not look very happy. "What's the matter, Mom? Are you afraid to get wet?" Meghan teased. "I'll bet you'll melt, just like the Wicked Witch of the West!"

Mrs. Millett didn't laugh at the joke. Instead, she told the kids that she wasn't felling well. She was too tired to drive to the water park.

Meghan and Jake were disappointed. "My mom has chronic fatigue syndrome," Meghan explained. "Her illness makes her really tired. She's still a great mom."

"Thank you, dear," said Mrs. Millett. "I'm too tired to drive, but I have an idea. You can make your own Waterland and I'll rest in the lawn chair."

Meghan and Jake set up three different sprinklers. They dragged the play slide over to the wading pool and aimed the sprinkler on the slide. Meghan and Jake got soaking wet. Mrs. Millett sat in a lawn chair and rested. The kids played all day.

"Thank you for being so understanding," Meghan's mom said. "Now I feel better, but I'm really hot! There's only one cure for that." She stood under the sprinkler with all her clothes on. She was drenched from head to toe.

Meghan laughed and said, "Now you have chronic wet syndrome." Mrs. Millett rewarded her daughter with a big, wet hug. It turned out to be a wonderful day after all, in the backyard waterland.

1. **Which sentence best tells the main idea of this story?**

   (A) Meghan's mom has chronic fatigue syndrome.

   (B) Jake and Meghan miss out on Waterland, but they make their own water park and have fun anyway.

   (C) Jake and Meghan cannot go to Waterland.

   (D) Sprinklers make a great backyard water park.

2. **Which of the following happened after the kids dragged the slide over to the pool?**

   (F) Jake arrived at Meghan's house.

   (G) Meghan and Jake set up three sprinklers

   (H) Meghan's mom stood in the sprinkler with her clothes on.

   (J) Meghan's mom was too tired to drive.

3. **How do you think Mrs. Millett feels about not being able to take the kids to Waterland?**

   (A) She's glad that she won't have to spend her whole day with kids.

   (B) She feels sorry for herself and is glad she got out of it.

   (C) She's disappointed that she can't take them.

   (D) She's hurt and confused.

STOP

TAKS Reading—Objective 4

The student will apply critical-thinking skills to analyze culturally diverse written texts.

(4.10) Reading/comprehension
The student comprehends selections using a variety of strategies.
The student is expected to

(H) draw inferences such as conclusions or generalizations and support them with text evidence [and experience] (4–8); and (*See page 31.*)

(J) distinguish fact and opinion in various texts (4–8). (*See page 32.*)

(4.11) Reading/literary response
The student expresses and supports responses to various types of texts. The student is expected to

(C) support responses by referring to relevant aspects of text [and his/her own experiences] (4–8); and (*See page 33.*)

(D) connect, compare, and contrast ideas, themes, and issues across text (4–8). (*See page 34.*)

(4.12) Reading/text structures/literary concepts.
The student analyzes the characteristics of various types of texts (genres).
The student is expected to

(B) recognize that authors organize information in specific ways (4–5). (*See page 35.*)

Reading/Comprehension

Objective 4

Expectation: *draw inferences such as conclusions or generalizations and support them with text evidence [and experience]*

The North Star

The North Star is one of the most famous stars. Its star name is *Polaris*. It is called the North Star because it shines almost directly over the North Pole. If you are at the North Pole, the North Star is overhead. As you travel farther south, the star seems lower in the sky. Only people in the Northern Hemisphere can see the North Star.

Because the North Star is always in the same spot in the sky, it has been used for years to give direction to people at night. Sailors used the North Star to navigate through the oceans.

Polaris, like all stars, is always moving. Thousands of years from now, another star will get to be the North Star. Vega was the North Star thousands of years before it moved out of position and Polaris became the North Star.

DIRECTIONS: Answer the questions based on the passage.

1. **The North Star might be one of the most famous stars because _____ .**
   - (A) it is near the North Pole
   - (B) it is always moving
   - (C) it is always in the same spot in the sky
   - (D) it is difficult to find in the sky

2. **Another star will someday get to be the North Star because _____ .**
   - (F) stars are always moving
   - (G) there are many stars in the sky
   - (H) Earth will turn to the South Pole
   - (J) scientists rename it every 50 years

3. **The name Polaris most likely comes from which name?**
   - (A) polecat
   - (B) polar bear
   - (C) Poland
   - (D) North Pole

4. **Only people in the _____ Hemisphere can see the North Star.**
   - (F) Eastern
   - (G) Western
   - (H) Northern
   - (J) Southern

STOP

Reading/Comprehension

Objective
4

Expectation: distinguish fact and opinion in various texts

Marie Curie

One of the greatest scientists of all time is Marie Curie. Marie Curie was born in Poland in 1867. She studied at a university in Paris and lived in France for most of her adult life. Along with her husband, Pierre Curie, she studied radioactivity. She was awarded the Nobel Prize in chemistry in 1911 for her work discovering radium and polonium.

The discovery of radium was a turning point in history. Some medical advances based on the research of the Curies are the x-ray and the use of radiation to treat cancer.

The Curies were both generous people. Even though they were poor for most of their lives, they did not patent any of their discoveries so that everyone could benefit from their research. Marie Curie died in 1934. The world should not forget her.

DIRECTIONS: Are the following statements facts or opinions? Write an **F** if the statement is a fact. Write an **O** if it is an opinion.

1. _____ **Marie Curie is one of the greatest scientists of all time.**

2. _____ **Marie Curie was awarded the Nobel Prize in chemistry in 1911.**

3. _____ **The Curies studied radioactivity.**

4. _____ **The discovery of radium was the most important turning point in history.**

5. _____ **The Curies did not patent any of their discoveries.**

6. _____ **The Curies were poor for most of their lives.**

7. _____ **The world should never forget the Curies.**

STOP

Reading/Literary Response

Objective
4

Expectation: support responses by referring to relevant aspects of text
[and his/her own experiences]

DIRECTIONS: Read the passage and answer the questions that follow.

> It's as black as ink out here in the pasture, and I'm as tired as an old shoe. But even if I were in my bed, I don't think I'd be sleeping like a baby tonight.
>
> Last summer for my birthday, my parents gave me my dream horse. Her name is Goldie. She is a beautiful palomino. I love to watch her gallop around the pasture. She runs like the wind and looks so carefree. I hope I'll see her run that way again.
>
> Yesterday, after I fed her, I forgot to close the door to the feed shed. She got into the grain and ate like a pig, which is very unhealthy for a horse. The veterinarian said I have to watch her like a hawk tonight to be sure she doesn't get colic. That's a very bad stomachache. Because he also said I should keep her moving, I have walked her around and around the pasture until I feel like we're on a merry-go-round.
>
> Now the sun is finally beginning to peek over the horizon, and Goldie seems content. I think she's going to be as good as new.

1. **What will the narrator most likely do the next time she feeds the horse?**

   (A) She will feed the horse too much.

   (B) She will make sure she closes the feed shed door.

   (C) She will give the horse plenty of water.

   (D) She will leave the feed shed open.

2. **How much experience do you think the narrator has with horses?**

   (F) Lots. She's probably owned many horses before.

   (G) This is probably her first horse. She doesn't have a lot of experience.

   (H) She's probably owned a horse before this, but not many.

   (J) I can't tell from the story.

3. **Based on the passage, which of the following is most likely true about the narrator?**

   (A) She really does not care much about Goldie.

   (B) She is devoted to Goldie and will be dedicated to helping her.

   (C) She will not want to have anything to do with horses in the future.

   (D) The story does not reveal anything about the narrator.

Reading/Literary Response

Objective 4

Expectation: connect, compare, and contrast ideas, themes, and issues across text

---

Walks All Over the Sky

Back when the sky was completely dark there was a chief with two sons, a younger son, One Who Walks All Over the Sky, and an older son, Walking About Early. The younger son was sad to see the sky always so dark so he made a mask out of wood and pitch (the Sun) and lit it on fire. Each day he travels across the sky. At night he sleeps below the horizon and when he snores sparks fly for the mask and make the stars. The older brother became jealous. To impress their father he smeared fat and charcoal on his face (the Moon) and makes his own path across the sky.

–From the *Tsimshian of the Pacific Northwest*

The Porcupine

Once Porcupine and Beaver argued about the seasons. Porcupine wanted five winter months. He held up one hand and showed his five fingers. He said, "Let the winter months be the same in number as the fingers on my hand." Beaver said, "No," and held up his tail, which had many cracks or scratches on it. He said, "Let the winter months be the same in number as the scratches on my tail." They argued more and Porcupine got angry and bit off his thumb. Then, holding up his hand with the four fingers, he said, "There must be only four winter months." Beaver was afraid and gave in. *For this reason, today porcupines have four claws on each foot.*

–From the *Tahltan: Teit, Journal of American Folk-Lore, xxxii, 226*

DIRECTIONS: Answer the questions based on the passages.

1. **What is the main idea of the first story?**

_____

_____

2. **What is the main idea of the second story?**

_____

_____

3. **In what ways are these two stories alike?**

_____

_____

_____

_____

_____

_____

STOP

Reading/Text Structures/Literary Concepts

Objective 4

Expectation: *recognize that authors organize information in specific ways*

Drama

A drama is a play performed by actors. A drama tells a story. Drama can be serious, funny, or sometimes both. There are three basic kinds of drama: tragedy, comedy, and melodrama.

A tragedy is a drama about a serious subject. Tragedies often deal with the meaning of life and how people treat each other. In a tragedy, the hero never solves his or her problem. The end of a tragedy is always sad. Often someone dies at the end of a tragedy. Good does not always win over evil.

A comedy is a drama that expresses feelings of joy. Comedy can also show very silly behavior. In many famous comedies, there are people who dress up like someone else and surprise others at the end of the play with who they really are. In a comedy, the problems are solved by the end of the play. Good wins over evil.

A melodrama is a drama that tells a story of good against evil. A melodrama features an evil villain who tries to destroy the good characters. Melodrama is like a tragedy because it has a serious subject. It is like a comedy because it has a good ending where the problems are solved.

Drama is believed to have begun in ancient Greece. Greeks performed their plays in outdoor theaters. Many of the Greek tragedies were about myths. Drama was later popular in many countries: Italy, England, Spain, France, India, China, and Japan. Today, drama is popular in practically every country in the world.

DIRECTIONS: Imagine you are writing a report about drama. Fill in the chart below with information about the three ways to classify dramas. Include at least three characteristics for each type.

Tragedy	Comedy	Melodrama

STOP

Objective

4

For pages 31–35

Mini-Test

DIRECTIONS: Read the passage, then answer the questions.

During the 1700s, America wanted to gain independence from the British. This caused many struggles between the two countries.

The British passed a law in 1765 that required legal papers and other items to have a tax stamp. It was called the Stamp Act. Colonists were forced to pay a fee for the stamp. Secret groups began to work against the requirement of the tax stamp. The law was finally taken away in 1766.

In 1767, the British passed the Townshend Acts. These acts forced people to pay fees for many items, such as tea, paper, glass, lead, and paint. This wasn't fair.

Colonists were furious. On December 16, 1773, they tossed 342 chests of tea over the sides of ships in Boston Harbor. This was later called the Boston Tea Party. Colonists had shown that they would not accept these laws.

1. **Which of the following sentences from the story states an opinion?**

   (A) The British passed a law in 1765 that required legal papers and other items to have a tax stamp.

   (B) The law was finally taken away in 1766.

   (C) This was later called the Boston tea party.

   (D) This wasn't fair.

2. **What caused the colonists to throw 342 chests of tea into Boston Harbor?**

   (F) They were angry about the Townshend Acts.

   (G) They wanted to make a big pot of tea.

   (H) The tea was bad.

   (J) They were angry because of the Stamp Act.

3. **According to the text, what was the cause of the many struggles?**

   (A) Secret groups began to work against the requirement of the tax stamp.

   (B) Colonists were forced to pay a fee for the stamp.

   (C) America wanted to gain independence from the British.

   (D) The British passed the Townshend Acts.

4. **How is this passage organized?**

   (F) by the names of the laws

   (G) in order of the year in which events happened

   (H) by comparing two unlike things

   (J) by the author's opinions of each event

STOP

How Am I Doing?

Objective 1 Mini-Test Page 13 **Number Correct** [ ]	**7** answers correct	**Great Job!** Move on to the section test on page 39.
	5–6 answers correct	**You're almost there!** But you still need a little practice. Review practice pages 8–12 before moving on to the section test on page 39.
	0–4 answers correct	**Oops!** Time to review what you have learned and try again. Review the practice section on pages 8–12. Then retake the test on page 13. Now move on to the section test on page 39.
Objective 2 Mini-Test Page 19 **Number Correct** [ ]	**6** answers correct	**Awesome!** Move on to the section test on page 39.
	4–5 answers correct	**You're almost there!** But you still need a little practice. Review practice pages 15–18 before moving on to the section test on page 39.
	0–3 answers correct	**Oops!** Time to review what you have learned and try again. Review the practice section on pages 15–18. Then retake the test on page 19. Now move on to the section test on page 39.

How Am I Doing?

Objective 3 Mini-Test Page 29 **Number Correct**	**3** answers correct	**Great Job!** Move on to the section test on page 39.
	2 answers correct	**You're almost there!** But you still need a little practice. Review practice pages 21–28 before moving on to the section test on page 39.
	0–1 answers correct	**Oops!** Time to review what you have learned and try again. Review the practice section on pages 21–28. Then retake the test on page 29. Now move on to the section test on page 39.
Objective 4 Mini-Test Page 36 **Number Correct**	**4** answers correct	**Awesome!** Move on to the section test on page 39.
	3 answers correct	**You're almost there!** But you still need a little practice. Review practice pages 31–35 before moving on to the section test on page 39.
	0–2 answers correct	**Oops!** Time to review what you have learned and try again. Review the practice section on pages 31–35. Then retake the test on page 36. Now move on to the section test on page 39.

Final Test for
Reading
for pages 8–36

DIRECTIONS: Choose the word that correctly completes both sentences.

1. **The player began to _____ .**
   Put the new _____ on the car.
   - (A) run
   - (B) fender
   - (C) weaken
   - (D) tire

2. **The sun _____ at 5:45.**
   A _____ grew beside the steps.
   - (F) appeared
   - (G) rose
   - (H) flower
   - (J) set

3. **My _____ is in the closet.**
   Add a new _____ of paint.
   - (A) hat
   - (B) color
   - (C) shirt
   - (D) coat

4. **Do you feel _____ ?**
   We get our water from a _____ .
   - (F) well
   - (G) good
   - (H) pipe
   - (J) sick

5. **Mrs. Johnson said Carrie was a _____ student.**
   The light from the headlights was _____ .
   - (A) noisy
   - (B) red
   - (C) bright
   - (D) hard working

DIRECTIONS: Choose the best answer.

6. **What prefix can you add to the root word *satisfied* to make a word that means "not satisfied."**
   - (F) *re-*
   - (G) *anti-*
   - (H) *dis-*
   - (J) *pre-*

7. **What prefix can you add to the root word *view* to make a word that means "to look at again."**
   - (A) *re-*
   - (B) *anti-*
   - (C) *dis-*
   - (D) *pre-*

GO

Name _____   Date _____

DIRECTIONS: Read the passage, then answer the questions.

Helping the Mountain Gorilla

Mountain gorillas live in the rain forests in Rwanda, Uganda, and the Democratic Republic of the Congo. These large, beautiful animals are becoming very rare. They have lost much of their habitat as people move in and take over gorillas' lands. Although there are strict laws protecting gorillas, poachers continue to hunt them.

Scientists observe gorillas to learn about their habits and needs. Then scientists write about their findings in magazines. Concerned readers sometimes contribute money to help safeguard the mountain gorillas.

Many other people are working hard to protect the mountain gorillas. Park rangers patrol the rain forest and arrest poachers. Tourists bring much-needed money into the area, encouraging local residents to protect the gorillas, too.

8. **What is this passage mainly about?**

   (F) mountain gorillas' family relationships

   (G) scientists who study mountain gorillas

   (H) ways that gorillas are threatened and helped

   (J) poachers and wars that threaten gorillas' survival

9. **Which words help you figure out the meaning of *habitat?***

   (A) "large, beautiful animals"

   (B) "gorillas' lands"

   (C) "the human population"

   (D) "recent civil wars"

10. **In this passage, *poacher* means _____ .**

    (F) park ranger

    (G) mountain gorilla

    (H) unlawful hunter

    (J) scientist

11. **The author of the passage thinks that tourism _____ .**

    (A) is very harmful to mountain gorillas

    (B) is one cause of civil wars in Africa

    (C) can be helpful to mountain gorillas

    (D) is one cause of overpopulation in Africa

12. **The author's purpose for writing this passage is _____ .**

    (F) to entertain readers

    (G) to inform readers about mountain gorillas

    (H) to motivate readers to visit Rwanda

    (J) to explain to readers where Africa is

13. **Which of the following is a fact?**

    (A) Mountain gorillas are beautiful animals.

    (B) Mountain gorillas live in the rain forests in Rwanda, Uganda, and the Democratic Republic of the Congo.

    (C) Everyone should send money to help the gorillas.

    (D) Scientists work to arrest poachers.

GO

Name _____   Date _____

DIRECTIONS: Read the passage, then answer the questions.

Home Alone

"Are you sure you're going to be all right at home alone?" Yong's mother asked.

"Yes, Mom," Yong replied, trying not to roll her eyes. "I'm old enough to stay here alone for three hours." Yong's mom and dad were going to a barbecue that afternoon. Since kids weren't invited, Yong was staying home alone. It was the first time her parents had left her home by herself. Yong was a little nervous, but she was sure she could handle it.

"Let me give you a last-minute quiz to make sure," her dad said. Yong's father was a teacher, and he was always giving her little tests. "What happens if somebody calls and asks for your mom or me?"

"I tell them that you are busy and can't come to the phone right now," Yong said. "Then I take a message."

"What if there is a knock on the door?" asked her dad.

"I don't answer it, because I can't let anyone in anyway."

"Okay, here's a tough one." Her father looked very serious. "What if you hear ghosts in the closets?"

"Dad!" Yong giggled. "Our house isn't haunted. I'll be fine. Look, I have the phone number of the house where you'll be, so I can call if I need to. I've got the numbers for the police, the fire department, and the poison control center. I won't turn on the stove or leave the house. And, I'll double lock the doors behind you when you leave."

Yong's parents were satisfied. They hugged her goodbye and left for the afternoon. Yong sat for a few minutes and enjoyed the quiet of the empty house. Then she went to the kitchen to fix herself a snack. She opened the cupboard door. Then she jumped back, startled. There was a ghost in the cupboard! Yong laughed and laughed. Her dad had taped up a picture of a ghost. It said, "BOO! We love you!"

14. **Which answer shows the best summary of this story?**

(F) Yong is staying home by herself for the first time and must remember all the important safety rules.

(G) Yong cannot go to the barbecue with her mom and dad.

(H) Yong's parents play a trick on her by hiding a paper ghost in the cupboard.

(J) Yong enjoys a peaceful afternoon at home alone.

15. **What is the setting of this story?**

(A) the beach

(B) a barbecue

(C) Yong's house

(D) a haunted house

16. **What is the main reason Yong's dad keeps asking her questions?**

(F) He wants to make sure she knows all the emergency phone numbers.

(G) He wants to make sure she will be safe while they are gone.

(H) He likes giving her quizzes.

(J) He played a trick on her.

17. **What should Yong do if someone knocks at the door?**

(A) She should answer it.

(B) She should call her dad.

(C) She should not answer it and not let anyone in.

(D) She should see who it is before letting the person in.

18. **What do you think Yong will do if she spills drain cleaner and the dog accidentally licks some up?**

(F) She will call her friend Sam to tell him.

(G) She will call the fire department.

(H) She will do nothing.

(J) She will call the poison control center and then her parents.

19. **Because kids are not invited to the barbecue,**

(A) they won't have any fun.

(B) the parents will not go.

(C) Yong must stay home alone.

(D) Yong will not get any dinner.

20. **Who are the main characters in this story?**

(F) Yong, her mom, and her dad

(G) Yong and her friend Sam

(H) Yong, her dad, and the dog

(J) Yong and her dad

21. **What do you learn about Yong's dad?**

(A) He has a good sense of humor.

(B) He is very serious.

(C) He is very quiet.

(D) He has a good job.

22. **Which of the following would NOT have been a logical ending for the story.**

(F) Yong enjoys her afternoon alone eating popcorn and watching a movie.

(G) Yong's parents decide to stay home because she doesn't want to be alone.

(H) Yong thinks of a good trick to play on her dad when he gets home.

(J) Yong's parents come home and find her fast asleep on the couch.

DIRECTIONS: Study the outline and then answer the questions.

Owls

    I. _____

        A. Great Horned Owl

        B. Snowy Owl

        C. Barn Owl

    II. Body Characteristics

        A. Size

        B. Body Covering

        C. _____

        D. Eyes, Talons, and Beaks

    III. Eating Habits

        A. Mice

        B. Other Small Rodents

23. **Which of the following fits best in the blank next to I.?**

(A) Owl Status

(B) Owl Habitats

(C) Types of Owls

(D) Owl Reproduction

24. **Which of the following fits best in the blank next to C.?**

(F) Feather Variations

(G) Grasses and Leaves

(H) Trees

(J) Nocturnal

Final Reading Test
Answer Sheet

1 (A) (B) (C) (D)
2 (F) (G) (H) (J)
3 (A) (B) (C) (D)
4 (F) (G) (H) (J)
5 (A) (B) (C) (D)
6 (F) (G) (H) (J)
7 (A) (B) (C) (D)
8 (F) (G) (H) (J)
9 (A) (B) (C) (D)
10 (F) (G) (H) (J)

11 (A) (B) (C) (D)
12 (F) (G) (H) (J)
13 (A) (B) (C) (D)
14 (F) (G) (H) (J)
15 (A) (B) (C) (D)
16 (F) (G) (H) (J)
17 (A) (B) (C) (D)
18 (F) (G) (H) (J)
19 (A) (B) (C) (D)
20 (F) (G) (H) (J)

21 (A) (B) (C) (D)
22 (F) (G) (H) (J)
23 (A) (B) (C) (D)
24 (F) (G) (H) (J)

TAKS Writing—Objective 1

The student will, within a given context, produce an effective composition for a specific purpose.

(4.15) Writing/purposes

The student writes for a variety of audiences and purposes and in a variety of forms. The student is expected to

(A) write to express, [discover, record,] develop, reflect on ideas, and to problem solve (4–8); (*See page 45.*)

(C) write to inform such as to explain, describe, [report,] and narrate (4–8); (*See page 46.*)

(D) write to entertain such as to compose [humorous poems or] short stories (4–8); and (*See page 47.*)

(E) exhibit an identifiable voice in personal narratives and in stories (4–5). (*See page 48.*)

What it means:

● *Voice* is the point of view from which a story is told. In first-person point of view, the narrator is a character in the story and uses the pronoun *I*. In third-person point of view, the narrator is an observer.

(4.16) Writing/penmanship/capitalization/punctuation

The student composes original texts, applying the conventions of written language such as capitalization, punctuation, and penmanship to communicate clearly. The student is expected to

(A) write legibly by selecting cursive or manuscript as appropriate (4–8).

(4.19) Writing/writing processes

The student selects and uses writing processes for self-initiated and assigned writing. The student is expected to

(C) revise selected drafts by adding, elaborating, deleting, combining, and rearranging text (4–8); and (*See page 49.*)

(D) revise drafts for coherence, progression, and logical support of ideas (4–8). (*See page 50.*)

Writing/Purposes

Objective 1

Expectation: write to express, [discover, record,] develop, reflect on ideas, and to problem solve

DIRECTIONS: Read the flyer that two girls designed to advertise their landscaping business. Then, think about what you could do around your neighborhood to make money. Write your answer to each question below.

Hire us to take care of your yard this summer.

We will mow, edge, water, and care for your flowers.

Our prices are reasonable.

We work hard.

We can give you letters from other neighbors who have used our yard services.

Call for more information!

Tina and Yani 123-4567

---

1. **Pick one thing you could do around your neighborhood to make money. Describe what you would do.**

   _____
   _____
   _____
   _____
   _____
   _____

2. **Why should your neighbors hire you to do this for them?**

   _____
   _____
   _____

3. **How would you convince your neighbors to hire you?**

   _____
   _____
   _____
   _____
   _____
   _____
   _____
   _____
   _____

STOP

Writing/Purposes

Objective
1

Expectation: *write to inform such as to explain, describe, [report,] and narrate*

DIRECTIONS: Read the paragraph below about how to plant a seed. Then, think of something you know how to do well. Write a paragraph that explains how to do it. Use words such as *first*, *next*, *then*, *finally*, and *last*.

I found out how to plant a seed and make it grow. First, I found a spot where the plant would get the right amount of sunshine. Next, I dug a hole, put the seed into the soil, and then covered the seed with soil. Then I watered the seed. After a couple weeks it began to grow into a beautiful plant.

_____

_____

_____

_____

_____

_____

_____

_____

_____

_____

_____

_____

_____

_____

_____

_____

STOP

Writing/Purposes

Objective
1

Expectation: *write to entertain such as to compose [humorous poems or]*
short stories

DIRECTIONS: Write a paragraph about the funniest thing that has ever happened to you. Give details that will help the readers feel like they were there, too.

_____

_____

_____

_____

_____

_____

_____

_____

_____

_____

_____

_____

_____

_____

_____

_____

_____

_____

_____

_____

_____

_____

STOP

Name _____ Date _____

Writing/Purposes

Objective 1

Expectation: *exhibit an identifiable voice in personal narratives and in stories*

DIRECTIONS: Write a paragraph about your favorite way to spend a day. Give details about why these activities are your favorites. Use words that express your feelings.

_____

_____

_____

_____

_____

_____

_____

_____

_____

_____

_____

_____

_____

_____

_____

_____

_____

_____

_____

_____

_____

_____

_____

Writing/Purposes

Objective 1

Expectation: revise selected drafts by adding, elaborating, deleting, combining, and rearranging text

DIRECTIONS: Read the report, then answer the questions.

(1) Thomas Jefferson accomplished many great things. (2) He is probably best known as the main author of the Declaration of Independence. (3) Jefferson was a person of integrity, and many people trusted him. (4) He was a member of the Continental Congress and a minister to France. (5) He was made Secretary of State in 1790 and Vice President in 1797. (6) Jefferson served as President of the United States from 1801 to 1809. (7) His wife was not alive to be his first lady. (8) This great man continued to work for his principles until he passed away in 1826.

1. **What is the topic sentence of the paragraph?**

   Ⓐ Sentence 1

   Ⓑ Sentence 2

   Ⓒ Sentence 3

   Ⓓ Sentence 4

2. **Which of these could be added after sentence 2?**

   Ⓕ Many politicians signed the Declaration.

   Ⓖ He was only 33 years old when he helped write the Declaration.

   Ⓗ The Declaration of Independence was the first step in a war against Britain.

   Ⓙ Benjamin Franklin helped Jefferson with some of the ideas in the document.

3. **Which sentence does not belong in the paragraph?**

   Ⓐ Sentence 5

   Ⓑ Sentence 6

   Ⓒ Sentence 7

   Ⓓ Sentence 8

4. **Which of these could be added after sentence 6?**

   Ⓕ He was president for seven years.

   Ⓖ During his presidency, he helped the United States purchase the Louisiana Territories.

   Ⓗ Some people liked him and some didn't.

   Ⓙ He was only the eighth President of the United States.

5. **Write a Sentence 9 to complete the paragraph.**

   _____

   _____

   _____

   _____

   _____

   _____

   _____

STOP

Writing/Purposes

Objective 1

Expectation: *revise drafts for coherence, progression, and logical support of ideas*

DIRECTIONS: Read the passage, then answer the questions.

(1) People in the city of Rabaul live in a huge volcanic crater. (2) Because of this, they know they need an escape plan in case of an eruption.

(3) In the fall of 1994, people began to notice signs of an eruption. (4) Recognized the signs. (5) Birds flew away from their nests; the ground shook in an up-and-down motion rather than side-to-side; and sea snakes slithered out of the ocean.

(6) On the day of the eruption, earthquakes shook Rabaul. (7) More than 50,000 people left the area. (8) Volcanic ash fills the sky.

(9) When the smoke cleared, about three-fourths of the houses on the island been flattened. (10) The island suffered greatly, but because of planning only a few people lost their lives.

1. How is sentence 2 best written?

- (A) They know they need an escape plan, because of this, in case of an eruption.
- (B) They know, because of this, that they need an escape plan in case of an eruption.
- (C) An escape plan in case of eruption because of this they need.
- (D) As it is

2. Which is not a complete sentence?

- (F) Sentence 1
- (G) Sentence 2
- (H) Sentence 3
- (J) Sentence 4

3. Which sentence could be added after sentence 5?

- (A) Animals can sense an earthquake long before people can feel the tremors.
- (B) Sea snakes are snakes that live in water.
- (C) The snakes slithered in a side-to-side motion.
- (D) The ocean nearby is filled with many creatures.

4. In sentence 9, *been* is best written _____ .

- (F) have been
- (G) beened
- (H) had been
- (J) As it is

5. In sentence 8, *fills* is best written

- (A) filled
- (B) filling
- (C) fills
- (D) As it is

STOP

Objective

1

Mini-Test

DIRECTIONS: Read the paragraph and answer the questions that follow.

Volcanoes

(1) There are more than 15,000 active volcanoes in the world. (2) Still, know everything there is to know about volcanoes scientists do not. (3) The study of volcanoes is called *volcanology*, and people who study volcanoes are called volcanologists.

(4) How does a volcano form? (5) Hot liquid rock, called magma, bubbles toward the surface through rock. (6) Once magma has arrived at the earth's surface, it is called *lava*. (7) Lava builds up until it forms a mountain in the shape of a cone. (8) The spot where lava comes up to the earth's surface through the cone is called a *volcano*.

(9) Some volcanic eruptions calm, but others destructive. (10) Large pieces of rock can be thrown out of the volcano. (11) People near an erupting volcano can be in great danger from flowing lava and volcanic bombs.

1. Sentence 2 is best written

Ⓐ Scientists still don't know everything there is to know about volcanoes.

Ⓑ Scientists don't know everything there is to know about volcanoes still.

Ⓒ Scientists don't still know everything there is to know about volcanoes.

Ⓓ As it is

2. Which of these is not a sentence?

Ⓕ Sentence 8

Ⓖ Sentence 9

Ⓗ Sentence 10

Ⓙ Sentence 11

3. Which sentence could be added after Sentence 10?

Ⓐ Some people collect these rocks after the eruption.

Ⓑ Dust is also thrown out and can cloud the air.

Ⓒ Rocks are also formed

Ⓓ Sometimes the rocks come out with so much force they are called volcanic bombs.

4. In Sentence 11, *flowing* is best written

Ⓕ flowdering

Ⓖ flowering

Ⓗ flowed

Ⓙ As it is

TAKS Writing—Objective 2

In addition to the organization and development of ideas, a successful writer applies the conventions of the English language in order to communicate clearly. The use of accurate capitalization, punctuation, spelling, grammar, usage, and sentence structure is vital to the reader's understanding of the text. The proficient writer also develops, refines, and successfully uses editing and proofreading skills to find and correct errors in his or her work. Objective 2 tests the student's command of conventions (appropriate to the grade level) in the production of a written composition.

The student will produce a piece of writing that demonstrates a command of the conventions of spelling, capitalization, punctuation, grammar, usage, and sentence structure.

(4.16)   Writing/penmanship/capitalization/punctuation
The student composes original texts, applying the conventions of written language such as capitalization, punctuation, and penmanship to communicate clearly. The student is expected to
  (B) capitalize and punctuate correctly to clarify and enhance meaning such as capitalizing titles, using possessives, commas in a series, commas in direct address, and sentence punctuation (4–5). (*See pages 53–54.*)

(4.17)   Writing/spelling
The student spells proficiently. The student is expected to
  (A) write with accurate spelling of syllable constructions, including closed, open, consonant before –*le*, and syllable boundary patterns (3–6); (*See page 55.*)
  (B) write with accurate spelling of roots such as *drink*, *speak, read*, or *happy*; inflections such as those that change tense or number; suffixes such as –*able* or –*less*; and prefixes such as *re* –or *un*– (4–6); and (*See page 56.*)
  (D) spell accurately in final drafts (4–8). (*See page 57.*)

(4.18)   Writing/grammar/usage
The student applies standard grammar and usage to communicate clearly and effectively in writing. The student is expected to
  (A) use regular and irregular plurals correctly (4–6); (*See page 58.*)
  (B) write in complete sentences, varying the types such as compound and complex to match meanings and purposes (4–5); (*See page 59.*)
  (C) employ standard English usage in writing for audiences, including subject-verb agreement, pronoun referents, and parts of speech (4–8); (*See page 60.*)
  (D) use adjectives (comparative and superlative forms) and adverbs appropriately to make writing vivid or precise (4–8); (*See page 61.*)
  (E) use prepositional phrases to elaborate written ideas (4–8); (*See page 62.*)
  (F) use conjunctions to connect ideas meaningfully (4–5); (*See page 63.*)
  (G) write with increasing accuracy when using apostrophes in contractions such as it's and possessives such as Jan's (4–8); and (*See page 64.*)
  (H) write with increasing accuracy when using objective case pronouns such as "Dan cooked for you and me." (4–5). (*See page 65.*)

(4.19)   Writing/writing processes
The student selects and uses writing processes for self-initiated and assigned writing. The student is expected to
  (E) edit drafts for specific purposes such as to ensure standard usage, varied sentence structure, and appropriate word choice (4–8); and (*See page 66.*)
  (H) proofread his/her own writing and that of others (4–8). (*See page 67.*)

Writing/Penmanship/Capitalization/Punctuation

Objective 2

Expectation: *capitalize and punctuate correctly to clarify and enhance meaning such as capitalizing titles, using possessives, commas in a series, commas in direct address, and sentence punctuation*

DIRECTIONS: Choose the part that does not have correct punctuation. If all the parts are correct, mark "None."

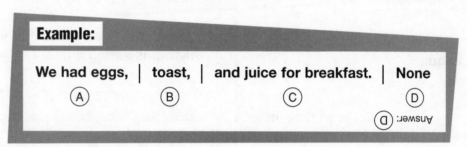

Example:

| We had eggs, | toast, | and juice for breakfast. | None |
| (A) | (B) | (C) | (D) |

Answer: (D)

1. Red, blue, | and green fireworks | lit up the sky. | None
   (A)   (B)   (C)   (D)

2. My friend | lives in | Miami Florida. | None
   (F)   (G)   (H)   (J)

3. Michael's grandmother | was born | on January 1, 1942. | None
   (A)   (B)   (C)   (D)

4. The driver knew | she was a few miles | from Houston Texas. | None
   (F)   (G)   (H)   (J)

5. Main Street School | had its first winter festival | on November 15 1983. | None
   (A)   (B)   (C)   (D)

6. We ate birthday cake | and sang songs | at the party. | None
   (F)   (G)   (H)   (J)

7. (A) Maria Hernandez

   (B) 126 Cherry Hill Road

   (C) Fresno California

   (D) None

GO

Writing/Penmanship/Capitalization/Punctuation

Objective 2

Expectation: capitalize and punctuate correctly to clarify and enhance meaning such as capitalizing titles, using possessives, commas in a series, commas in direct address, and sentence punctuation

DIRECTIONS: Circle the word in parentheses that correctly fits the sentence.

8. The _____ leaves were just beginning to bud.
(tree's, trees)

9. _____ watercolor won first prize in the contest.
(Beths', Beth's)

10. The _____ whiskers twitched as it sniffed the air.
(squirrels's, squirrel's)

11. My _____ purr is so loud it sounds like a motor.
(cats', cat's)

12. Her baby _____ name is Matthew.
(brothers', brother's)

13. The _____ scales glimmered in the water.
(fishes's, fish's)

14. The _____ light filtered through the trees.
(suns', sun's)

15. The school _____ lights flashed as it came to a stop.
(busses, bus's)

16. As we entered the old mansion, the _____ hinge creaked loudly.
(door's, doors')

DIRECTIONS: Rewrite each sentence, adding commas where necessary.

17. Jennifer did you know that your Venus flytrap is eating a fly?

_____

_____

18. I think Teresa that we should take my flytrap to the class picnic.

_____

_____

19. Tony why does your science project include next year's calendar and all those mirrors?

_____

_____

_____

20. To tell you the truth Joe I'm trying to find a way to see into the future.

_____

_____

21. Is the electric whatzit machine I made running Rebecca?

_____

STOP

Writing/Spelling

Objective 2

Expectation: *write with accurate spelling of syllable constructions, including closed, open, consonant before –le, and syllable boundary patterns*

Below are some of the rules for dividing words into syllables:

1. **Closed:** These syllables end in a consonant. The vowel sound is generally short. (Examples: *rab/bit, nap/kin*)

2. **Open:** These syllables end in a vowel. The vowel sound is usually long. (Examples: *ti/ger, pi/lot*)

3. **Vowel-silent e:** These generally represent long-vowel sounds. (Examples: *com/pete, de/cide*)

4. **Consonant -le:** Usually when -le appears at the end of a word and a consonant comes before it, the consonant plus -le make up the last syllable. (Examples: *ta/ble, sta/ble*)

DIRECTIONS: Rewrite the following words divided into syllables.

1. addition

_____

2. another

_____

3. circus

_____

4. clothing

_____

5. couple

_____

6. decorate

_____

7. destroy

_____

8. double

_____

9. finger

_____

10. happen

_____

11. height

_____

12. ledge

_____

STOP

Name _____ Date _____

Writing/Spelling

Objective 2

Expectation: *write with accurate spelling of roots such as* drink, speak, read, *or* happy; *inflections such as those that change tense or number; suffixes such as –able or –less; and prefixes such as re– or un–*

DIRECTIONS: Write the plural of the following words.

1. man

_____

2. half

_____

3. tooth

_____

4. foot

_____

5. fly

_____

DIRECTIONS: Find the phrase that has a word spelled incorrectly.

6. Ⓐ traffic sounds
   Ⓑ five minutes
   Ⓒ amazing student
   Ⓓ loud grone

7. Ⓕ draw concloosions
   Ⓖ curious cat
   Ⓗ disappointing day
   Ⓙ make comparisons

8. Ⓐ excited kids
   Ⓑ venomous snakes
   Ⓒ dog hare
   Ⓓ detect sound

9. Ⓕ pioneer town
   Ⓖ save mony
   Ⓗ fine seafood
   Ⓙ rescue boat

10. Ⓐ mountain gorila
    Ⓑ crisp lettuce
    Ⓒ porcupine quills
    Ⓓ large building

DIRECTIONS: Find the underlined word that is not spelled correctly.

11. Ⓕ <u>identifable</u> a bird
    Ⓖ <u>bottle</u> of juice
    Ⓗ <u>quiet</u> room
    Ⓙ All correct

12. Ⓐ <u>easy</u> lesson
    Ⓑ last <u>forevr</u>
    Ⓒ paddle a <u>canoe</u>
    Ⓓ All correct

13. Ⓕ <u>unbalanced</u> tires
    Ⓖ <u>delicious</u> stew
    Ⓗ private <u>property</u>
    Ⓙ All correct

14. Ⓐ great <u>relief</u>
    Ⓑ our <u>mayor</u>
    Ⓒ <u>sunnie</u> day
    Ⓓ <u>drinking</u> water

Writing/Spelling

Objective 2   *Expectation:* spell accurately in final drafts

DIRECTIONS: Choose the word that completes the sentence and is spelled correctly.

1. **The garage needed a _____ cleaning.**
   - (A) thoroh
   - (B) thurow
   - (C) thourough
   - (D) thorough

2. **That is the _____ story I've ever read.**
   - (F) funniest
   - (G) funnyest
   - (H) funnyst
   - (J) funnest

3. **I grew three _____ this year.**
   - (A) inchs
   - (B) inchys
   - (C) inchies
   - (D) inches

4. **We planted _____ along the fence.**
   - (F) daisyes
   - (G) daisies
   - (H) daisys
   - (J) daises

5. **My brother _____ the coolest gift.**
   - (A) recieved
   - (B) receeved
   - (C) received
   - (D) receaved

6. **I _____ at the store after school.**
   - (F) stopt
   - (G) stoped
   - (H) stoppt
   - (J) stopped

7. **He is my best _____.**
   - (A) frind
   - (B) frend
   - (C) friend
   - (D) fiend

8. **Miss Lambert was _____ about the litter on her lawn.**
   - (F) fuious
   - (G) furious
   - (H) furius
   - (J) fiurius

9. **I can't _____ it!**
   - (A) belive
   - (B) believe
   - (C) beleive
   - (D) beleve

10. **Her cousin is the most _____ person I've ever met.**
    - (F) polight
    - (G) pollite
    - (H) pollight
    - (J) polite

STOP

Writing/Grammar/Usage

Objective
2

Expectation: *use regular and irregular plurals correctly*

DIRECTIONS: Change the following singular nouns to plural nouns.

1. dinosaur _____

2. stone _____

3. ranch _____

4. yard _____

5. foot _____

6. thermometer _____

7. walrus _____

8. sandwich _____

9. man _____

10. zebra _____

11. glass _____

12. German _____

13. ostrich _____

14. helicopter _____

15. crown _____

16. refrigerator _____

17. turtle _____

18. tooth _____

19. pitcher _____

20. ax _____

21. child _____

22. goose _____

23. cheese _____

24. boy _____

25. village _____

26. brush _____

27. thumb _____

28. movie _____

29. library _____

30. city _____

DIRECTIONS: Write three sentences about a city mouse and his cousins who come to visit from the country. Remember to use plurals correctly.

31. _____

_____

_____

_____

_____

_____

STOP

58

Writing/Grammar/Usage

Objective 2

Expectation: write in complete sentences, varying the types such as compound and complex to match meanings and purposes

---

DIRECTIONS: Write **S** before each line that is a sentence. Write **F** before each line that is a fragment.

1. _____ You should know better.

2. _____ Walking faster all the time.

3. _____ Wait outside.

4. _____ Caught the ball and threw it to second base.

5. _____ Every house in town.

6. _____ Sit quietly.

7. _____ They will arrive soon.

8. _____ Close the window.

9. _____ A few people in this club.

10. _____ Today during lunch.

11. _____ He can read well.

12. _____ Swimming against the strong current.

13. _____ Looks like mine.

14. _____ The dog jumped the fence easily.

15. _____ Harold and the other boys on the team.

16. _____ Those girls moved here from Akron.

DIRECTIONS: Choose the answer that best combines the underlined sentences.

17. **Pedro finished his homework.**
    Pedro went to bed.
    - (A) Pedro finished his homework or went to bed.
    - (B) Pedro finished his homework then went to bed.
    - (C) Pedro finished his homework because he went to bed.
    - (D) Going to bed, Pedro finished his homework

18. **The truck brought the furniture to our house.**
    The truck was large.
    - (F) The large truck, which brought the furniture to our house.
    - (G) The truck was large that brought the furniture to our house.
    - (H) The truck brought the furniture to our house, and was large.
    - (J) The large truck brought the furniture to our house.

19. **Arnie found a ball.**
    The ball was red.
    He found it on the way to school.
    - (A) Finding a red ball, Arnie was on his way to school.
    - (B) Arnie found a red ball on the way to school.
    - (C) Arnie found a ball on the way to school that was red.
    - (D) The red ball that Arnie found on the way to school.

STOP

Writing/Grammar/Usage

Objective 2

Expectation: employ standard English usage in writing for audiences, including subject-verb agreement, pronoun referents, and parts of speech

---

DIRECTIONS: Choose the answer that completes the sentence best.

1. **Chang and Audrey made _____ kites together.**
   - (A) him
   - (B) she
   - (C) them
   - (D) their

2. **Are _____ parents coming to the concert?**
   - (F) she
   - (G) he
   - (H) her
   - (J) it

3. **_____ spoke to my mother on Parents' Night.**
   - (A) Him
   - (B) He
   - (C) Us
   - (D) Them

DIRECTIONS: Choose the answer that could replace the underlined word or words.

4. **<u>Jill and Keisha</u> went to soccer practice.**
   - (F) Him
   - (G) Them
   - (H) They
   - (J) She

5. **Did <u>Brian</u> find his lost cat?**
   - (A) him
   - (B) he
   - (C) it
   - (D) us

DIRECTIONS: Write a proper noun for each common noun. Write a common noun for each proper noun.

6. **country** _____

7. **boy** _____

8. **lake** _____

9. **California** _____

DIRECTIONS: Draw a line under each noun. Circle each pronoun.

10. **Yolanda walked her sister to school.**

11. **Karen and I played volleyball with our friends.**

12. **My father and Uncle Ken attended their club meeting.**

13. **Toby made a new dress.**

14. **Randy and Father are planting corn seeds.**

STOP

Writing/Grammar/Usage

Objective 2

Expectation: use adjectives (comparative and superlative forms) and adverbs appropriately to make writing vivid or precise

 Clue   An adjective is a word that describes a noun or pronoun.

DIRECTIONS: Circle the adjective(s) in each sentence.

1. Yolanda picked red and yellow roses from her garden.

2. Those pupils passed their spelling test.

3. This man is our new teacher.

4. Both children attended the birthday party.

5. My parents are busy people.

6. Spot is a playful, frisky dog.

7. Please sharpen these pencils, Frank.

8. Rudy hit two home runs in that game.

9. Judy bought two peaches and one red apple.

10. My kite glided through the bright blue sky.

11. Ira moved to the smallest town in Montana.

12. There are twelve boys and fourteen girls in Kit's class.

13. Devon read his book under the shady elm tree.

 Clue   An adverb is a word that describes a verb, adjective, or another adverb. It usually tells when, how, where, or how often something is done.

DIRECTIONS: Circle the adverb in each sentence.

14. Jerry behaved badly.

15. The rain fell gently.

16. I will surely pass the test.

17. The children sang happily.

18. The stream rushed by swiftly.

19. Jill came by early.

20. The stars glittered brightly.

21. The neighbors' dog barked loudly.

22. Mr. Ito drove carefully.

STOP

Writing/Grammar/Usage

Objective 2

Expectation: *use prepositional phrases to elaborate written ideas*

DIRECTIONS: Underline each prepositional phrase in the sentence below.

Example:

Jill's skates were left out <u>in the rain</u>.

1. The rubies in the safe are priceless.

2. The telephone rang four times during lunch.

3. Here is a surprise for you.

4. She put her toys in the closet.

5. The class enjoyed seeing Egyptian treasures at the museum.

6. The person with the lowest score wins.

7. He put the note on the refrigerator.

8. The lost watch was under the couch.

9. The high jumper went over the bar on his second try.

10. The troop with the most badges got a pizza party.

DIRECTIONS: Add a prepositional phrase to each sentence and rewrite it on the lines provided.

11. Sue ran yesterday.

_____

_____

12. Kim searched the garage.

_____

_____

13. Lisa stopped the car.

_____

_____

14. Krisha looked puzzled.

_____

_____

15. Stan took his canoe.

_____

_____

16. Ahmed ran the race.

_____

_____

17. The hail pelted the roof.

_____

_____

18. Jordan stopped and laughed.

_____

_____

STOP

Writing/Grammar/Usage

Objective 2

Expectation: *use conjunctions to connect ideas meaningfully*

DIRECTIONS: Choose the answer that best combines the underlined sentences.

1. **The tiny squirrel peeked from behind the tree.**
   The tiny squirrel scurried away.

   Ⓐ The tiny squirrel peeked and scurried away from behind the tree.

   Ⓑ The tiny squirrel peeked from behind the tree; it scurried away.

   Ⓒ The tiny squirrel peeked from behind the tree and scurried away.

   Ⓓ The tiny squirrel peeked from behind the tree and the tiny squirrel scurried away.

2. **Maxine arrived at 6 o'clock.**
   Sylvia arrived at 6 o'clock.

   Ⓕ Maxine arrived at 6 o'clock; so did Sylvia.

   Ⓖ Maxine arrived at 6 o'clock and Sylvia arrived at 6 o'clock.

   Ⓗ Maxine arrived at 6 o'clock, as did Sylvia.

   Ⓙ Maxine and Sylvia arrived at 6 o'clock.

3. **Janie has a bicycle.**
   Her bike is shiny. Her bike is green.

   Ⓐ Janie has a bicycle. It is shiny and green.

   Ⓑ Janie has a shiny green bicycle.

   Ⓒ Janie has a shiny bicycle. Janie has a green bicycle.

   Ⓓ Janie has a bicycle, which is shiny and green.

DIRECTIONS: Use a conjunction to make the following pairs of sentences one sentence. Write the new sentence on the lines.

4. **Tom wanted to be at the meeting. He had another appointment.**

   _____

   _____

5. **Marielle goes to dance class every Wednesday morning. Trina goes to dance class every Wednesday morning.**

   _____

   _____

   _____

6. **Hunter is deciding whether to go to Space Camp this summer. Hunter is deciding whether to go to Space Camp this fall.**

   _____

   _____

   _____

7. **The test was very difficult. I think I did well.**

   _____

   _____

8. **Grandma brought the presents for the party. Grandma brought the decorations for the party.**

   _____

   _____

STOP

Writing/Grammar/Usage

Objective 2 *Expectation: write with increasing accuracy when using apostrophes in contractions such as* it's *and possessives such as* Jan's

---

DIRECTIONS: Choose the words that form the contractions.

1. **Tiffany knew she shouldn't go near the deserted old house.**
   - (A) shall not
   - (B) should not
   - (C) will not
   - (D) could not

2. **"Don't even think about going near there," Mom told her.**
   - (F) do not
   - (G) did not
   - (H) does not
   - (J) will not

3. **"There aren't such things as ghosts," Tiffany replied.**
   - (A) were not
   - (B) could not
   - (C) are not
   - (D) cannot

DIRECTIONS: Write the words that form each contraction.

4. **"It doesn't matter," Mom replied.**

   _____

5. **As Tiffany walked past the house one night, she couldn't help noticing the odd sounds coming from it.**

   _____

6. **The sounds weren't like any other she had ever heard.**

   _____

7. **"I mustn't get too close," Tiffany thought as she crept up to the house.**

   _____

8. **"E-E-O-I-O-W!" Tiffany didn't move as she saw angry cats race past her.**

   _____

DIRECTIONS: Write the possessive form of each underlined word.

9. **The <u>children</u> section of the library is always busy.**

   _____

10. **The <u>frogs</u> pond was peaceful that night.**

    _____

11. **Can you see the <u>campers</u> tent from here?**

    _____

12. **There is a sale in the <u>men</u> section of the store today.**

    _____

13. **At the back of the farmhouse, we could see the <u>horses</u> paddock.**

Writing/Grammar/Usage

Objective 2

Expectation: write with increasing accuracy when using objective case pronouns such as "Dan cooked for you and me"

DIRECTIONS: Circle the correct pronoun from the parentheses at the end of each sentence.

1. Samantha and _____ were in the choir together.
   (she, her)

2. Between you and _____ , I don't think Shane's model boat will float.
   (I, me)

3. Mom made my friend and _____ peanut butter sandwiches for lunch.
   (I, me)

4. It was _____ who won the contest, not Marcus.
   (she, her)

5. It is _____ who always cleans the litter box.
   (I, me)

6. Ashley thinks Aaron and _____ are the best dancers.
   (she, her)

7. If I were _____, I would choose the red bike as my prize. (him, he)

8. _____ students have to work hard today so that we can go on our field trip tomorrow.
   (Us, We)

9. Call Shari and _____ if you decide you want to go with us.
   (I, me)

10. The chocolate cake was supposed to be for _____ boys only.
    (us, we)

11. Please bring the tickets for Stan and _____.
    (I, me)

12. Joni and _____ will be ready for the concert at 7:00.
    (I, me)

13. Thanks to _____ and Victor, we will have fish for dinner tonight.
    (her, she)

14. _____ and Bruce will be the first two up to bat.
    (Him, He)

15. Jamal and _____ were not at practice this week.
    (them, they)

STOP

Writing/Writing Processes

Objective
2

Expectation: edit drafts for specific purposes such as to ensure standard usage, varied sentence structure, and appropriate word choice

DIRECTIONS: Read the letter, then answer the questions. If the sentence needs no changes, choose "Correct as is."

Dear Ms. Wood:

(1) Our whole class would like to thank you for the nature trail tour. **(2)** We was amazed at the number of flowers, and animals, on the trail. **(3)** The birds and animals, all of them that we saw, were so beautiful. **(4)** We drew pictures of some of the birds and animals after we got back to school. **(5)** The wildflowers, which we saw on the nature trail, were colorful and interesting. **(6)** Our favorite was the one called Queen Anne's lace. **(7)** We are sending you a drawing of this flower as a thank you for the tour.

Sincerely,

Mrs. Jasper's Third Grade Class

1. Sentence 2 is best written—

(A) We were amazed by the number of flowers and animals on the trail.

(B) The flowers and animals was amazing on the trail.

(C) We were amazed at the number of flowers and animals on the trail.

(D) Correct as is

2. Sentence 3 is best written—

(F) The birds and animals that we seen were so beautiful.

(G) All of the birds and animals that we saw were so beautiful.

(H) All of the birds and all of the animals we saw were so beautiful.

(J) Correct as is

3. Sentence 5 is best written—

(A) The wildflowers that we saw on the nature trail were colorful and interesting.

(B) We saw on the trail wildflowers which were colorful and interesting.

(C) Wildflowers, colorful and interesting, which we saw on the trail.

(D) Correct as is

Writing/Writing Processes

Objective 2

Expectation: proofread his/her own writing and that of others

---

DIRECTIONS: Read each sentence. Choose the sentence that shows correct punctuation and capitalization. If the underlined part is correct, choose "Correct as is."

1. **The last thing I meant to do was <u>annoy the Andersons on arbor day</u>.**

   (A) annoy the andersons on arbor day

   (B) Annoy The Andersons on arbor day

   (C) annoy the Andersons on Arbor Day

   (D) Correct as is

2. **<u>New zealand</u> is home to a playful bird called the kea.**

   (F) New, Zealand

   (G) new zealand

   (H) New Zealand

   (J) Correct as is

DIRECTIONS: Choose the best answer.

3. **Either the garage or the porch must have _____ roof repaired this fall.**

   (A) their

   (B) its

   (C) that

   (D) they're

4. **Neither Julie nor Anna will bring _____ pager to class again.**

   (F) their

   (G) her

   (H) its

   (J) Correct as is

DIRECTIONS: Read the passage. Choose the answer that shows the best way to write the underlined section. If the underlined section is correct, choose "Correct as is."

People who live in <u>Nova Scotia Canada</u> (5) are called Bluenoses. This <u>isnt</u> (6) because of the color of their noses, however. This part of <u>Canada</u> (7) once sold large quantities of potatoes called bluenose potatoes. The potatoes got their name because each one had a blue end or <u>"nose."</u> (8)

5. (A) Nova Scotia, Canada

   (B) Nova Scotia, Canada,

   (C) Nova Scotia, canada

   (D) Correct as is

6. (F) isnt'

   (G) is'nt

   (H) isn't

   (J) Correct as is

7. (A) canada

   (B) Canada,

   (C) , Canada

   (D) Correct as is

8. (F) "nose.'

   (G) "nose".

   (H) 'nose.'

   (J) Correct as is

Objective

2

Mini-Test

DIRECTIONS: Choose the correct plural of each word.

1. grocery

- (A) grocerys
- (B) groceries
- (C) groceris
- (D) groceri

2. firefly

- (F) fireflies
- (G) fireflys
- (H) fireflyes
- (J) firefly

3. mouse

- (A) mouses
- (B) mousen
- (C) mice
- (D) mices

4. person

- (F) persona
- (G) people
- (H) peoples
- (J) personus

DIRECTIONS: Choose a proper noun to replace each common noun. Choose a common noun to replace each proper noun.

5. France

- (A) Paris
- (B) tower
- (C) country
- (D) travel

6. street

- (F) avenue
- (G) Maple Street
- (H) road
- (J) house

7. school

- (A) library
- (B) junior
- (C) Kellog Elementary
- (D) books

8. Mrs. Francis

- (F) principal
- (G) wagon
- (H) Brenda
- (J) school

DIRECTIONS: Choose the title that is correctly capitalized.

9. there are rocks in my socks

- (A) There are Rocks in My Socks
- (B) There Are Rocks in My Socks
- (C) There are Rocks in my Socks
- (D) There Are Rocks In My Socks

10. gus was a friendly mule

- (F) Gus Was a friendly mule
- (G) Gus was a Friendly Mule
- (H) Gus Was A Friendly Mule
- (J) Gus Was a Friendly Mule

TAKS Writing—Objective 3

Revision is an integral part of the writing process. After the first draft the competent writer often adds, deletes, combines, and/or rearranges words and sentences to better organize and more fully develop his or her thoughts and ideas. Objective 3 tests the student's ability to recognize and correct errors in organization and development in the context of peer-editing passages.

The student will recognize appropriate organization of ideas in written text.

(4.19) Writing/writing processes

The student selects and uses writing processes for self-initiated and assigned writing. The student is expected to

- **(C)** revise selected drafts by adding, elaborating, deleting, combining, and rearranging text (4–8); and (*See page 70.*)
- **(D)** revise drafts for coherence, progression, and logical support of ideas (4–8). (*See page 71.*)

Writing/Writing Processes

Objective
3

Expectation: *revise selected drafts by adding, elaborating, deleting, combining, and rearranging text*

DIRECTIONS: Read the passage and answer the questions.

(1) Serious storms are hurricanes that occur over the ocean. (2) The warm tropical ocean water is warm. (3) A low-pressure area forms above the waves, just as these areas often form during the summer and early fall. (4) The warm air zips up above the waves. (5) The moist air zips above the waves. (6) Cooler air in. (7) This causes the air to spin. (8) Air pressure in the center drops. (9) More warm, moist air is sucked up into the system. (10) It creates wind, rain, and clouds. (11) Inside the wall, the system's eye is calm. (12) But around the eye, the rain, wind, and clouds swirl in the fierce hurricane.

1. Sentence 1 is best written —

(A) Serious storms that occur over the ocean are hurricanes.

(B) Serious storms, hurricanes, occur over the ocean.

(C) Hurricanes are serious storms that occur over the ocean.

(D) As it is

2. Which sentence incorrectly repeats a word or group of words?

(F) Sentence 1

(G) Sentence 2

(H) Sentence 3

(J) Sentence 4

3. Which of these is not a sentence?

(A) Sentence 2

(B) Sentence 6

(C) Sentence 9

(D) Sentence 11

4. How can sentences 4 and 5 best be joined without changing their meanings?

(F) Zipping up above the waves, the water is warm and moist.

(G) The warm and moist air zips up above the waves.

(H) The warm air and the moist air zips up above the waves.

(J) The warm, moist air zips up above the waves.

Writing/Writing Processes

Objective 3

Expectation: *revise drafts for coherence, progression, and logical support of ideas*

DIRECTIONS: Read the passage and answer the questions that follow.

(1) Adding a new room is one of the most popular home improvements. (2) Another favorite improvement is increasing the size of the kitchen. (3) This is a good idea because families spend so much time in the kitchen. (4) For the outside of a house, building a deck is the number one improvement. (5) A deck is usually made of specially treated wood that can stand up to all kinds of weather.

1. Choose the best first sentence for this paragraph.

- (A) Buying a new home can be expensive.
- (B) When you add a room, it is usually one the whole family can use.
- (C) Families often outgrow their house.
- (D) Many people make improvements to an old home rather than buying a new one.

2. Which sentence should be left out of this paragraph?

- (F) Sentence 1
- (G) Sentence 3
- (H) Sentence 4
- (J) Sentence 5

DIRECTIONS: Choose the best topic sentence for each paragraph.

3. _____. Soap was once money to the people of Mexico. Lumps of coal were used as coins by the people of England. Stone money was used on the Pacific Ocean island of Yep. Even food has been used as money. In Russia, "coins" of cheese could be used to buy things.

- (A) Soap can be made from animal fat.
- (B) Soap is often used to wash children's mouths out.
- (C) Money was not always made of metals or paper, as it is today.
- (D) Money has been around for a long time.

4. _____. She installs computer systems in doctors' offices. After learning about each doctor's practice, she decides what kind of computer and programs will be best.

- (F) Many doctors have computers in their offices.
- (G) Many exciting jobs are available in the computer field.
- (H) Samantha's mother went to college to become an engineer.
- (J) Samantha's mother has an interesting job.

STOP

Objective

3

Mini-Test

DIRECTIONS: Read the paragraph. Choose the sentence that does not belong.

1. (1) Niagara Falls, one of the world's biggest waterfalls, is partly in the United States and partly in Canada. (2) My family went there for our vacation last summer. (3) In 1969, scientists did a strange thing at the falls. (4) They shut off the American falls for several months by building a big dam across the river so no water could get to the falls. (5) The scientists wanted to study the rocks underneath the water.

   (A) Sentence 1

   (B) Sentence 2

   (C) Sentence 4

   (D) Sentence 5

DIRECTIONS: Read the paragraph. Choose the sentence that fits best in the blank.

2. **One of the nicest things about summer evenings is being able to watch fireflies or try to catch them. _____. Some scientists think the lights are used to scare away birds that might eat the fireflies. Others think the fireflies use their lights to say "Hello" to their future mates.**

   (F) My grandma likes to sit on the porch in the evening.

   (G) I usually catch fireflies in a big jar.

   (H) Fireflies need to have lots of air if you catch them and put them in a jar.

   (J) Did you ever wonder why fireflies light up?

DIRECTIONS: Read the paragraph. Choose the best topic sentence for the paragraph.

3. **_____. This scientist found out that cars painted pink or any light shade seem to be safer. The light colors are more easily seen. Cars of two or three different colors may be even safer.**

   (A) Cars can come in many colors.

   (B) I prefer my cars to be red.

   (C) Scientists studied car accidents to look for ways to prevent them.

   (D) Scientists study natural phenomenon.

DIRECTIONS: Choose the answer that best develops the topic sentence below.

4. **The Gulf Stream is made up of a flow of warm ocean water a thousand times as great as the flow of the Amazon River.**

   (F) Scientists have mapped the Gulf Stream's course up the Atlantic Coast.

   (G) Hot springs also have warm water.

   (H) The Amazon River is in South America.

   (J) Water also flows down rivers and streams toward the oceans.

TAKS Writing—Objective 4

Editing and proofreading are also an important part of the writing process. During this stage the skillful writer uses correct sentence structure to ensure that his or her meaning is evident. Faulty phrasing, misuse of conjunctions, fragments, and run-on sentences can lead to confusion and misunderstanding of the intended message. Objective 4 tests the student's ability to recognize and correct errors in sentence structure in the context of peer-editing passages.

The student will recognize correct and effective sentence construction in written text.

(4.18) Writing/grammar/usage
The student applies standard grammar and usage to communicate clearly and effectively in writing. The student is expected to
- **(B)** write in complete sentences, varying the types such as compound and complex to match meanings and purposes (4–5); (*See page 74.*)
- **(E)** use prepositional phrases to elaborate written ideas (4–8);and (*See page 75.*)
- **(F)** use conjunctions to connect ideas meaningfully (4–5). (*See page 76.*)

(4.19) Writing/writing processes
The student selects and uses writing processes for self-initiated and assigned writing. The student is expected to
- **(E)** edit drafts for specific purposes such as to ensure standard usage, varied sentence structure, and appropriate word choice (4–8). (*See page 77.*)

Writing/Grammar/Usage

Objective 4

Expectation: *write in complete sentences, varying the types such as compound and complex to match meaning and purpose*

DIRECTIONS: Rewrite each run-on sentence to make it correct. Write **C** if each pair of sentences below is correct as is.

1. **Let's ask David to come with us. He knows about a great bike trail.**

   _____

   _____

2. **I can ride faster than you can let's race to the stop sign.**

   _____

   _____

3. **I'm thirsty does anyone have some bottled water?**

   _____

   _____

4. **We need to be careful on the bike trail in-line skaters can appear fast.**

   _____

   _____

5. **Do you know how to recognize a happy bicyclist? He has bugs in his teeth.**

   _____

   _____

6. **I love the playground it has great swings.**

   _____

   _____

7. **When I swing too high, I get sick do you?**

   _____

   _____

8. **I like the slide the best. I've always liked slides.**

   _____

   _____

9. **This ride was fun let's do it again tomorrow.**

   _____

   _____

DIRECTIONS: Rewrite each sentence fragment below to make it a sentence.

10. **found a hidden staircase in the old house**

    _____

    _____

11. **a mysterious note**

    _____

    _____

12. **lay behind the creaking door**

    _____

    _____

13. **the solution to the mystery**

    _____

    _____

Writing/Grammar/Usage

Objective 4

Expectation: *use prepositional phrases to elaborate written ideas*

DIRECTIONS: Underline each prepositional phrase in the sentences below.

1. The watch was still in the box.

2. The children's artwork is displayed at city hall.

3. The cat's food dish is under the bag.

4. Last Friday was the due date for the library book.

5. The singer bowed to the applause of the crowd.

6. Second place went to the girls' volleyball team.

7. My ten-speed bike is first on the list.

8. The baby's bottle was in the dishwasher.

9. The bat cracked in half when he hit the ball over the fence.

10. The prize went to the class with the best attendance.

DIRECTIONS: Add a prepositional phrase to each sentence and rewrite it on the line provided.

11. Mike called yesterday.

   _____

   _____

12. Kim searched the garage.

   _____

   _____

13. Lisa stopped the car.

   _____

   _____

14. Kira looked puzzled.

   _____

   _____

15. Peter took his canoe.

   _____

   _____

16. Ahmed ran the race.

   _____

   _____

17. The hail pelted the roof.

   _____

   _____

18. Jordan stopped and laughed.

   _____

STOP

Name _____ Date _____

Writing/Grammar/Usage

Objective
4

Expectation: *use conjunctions to connect ideas meaningfully*

DIRECTIONS: Use conjunctions to combine each set of three sentences into one sentence.

1. Horses can walk.
   Horses can trot.
   Horses can gallop.

   _____

   _____

   _____

2. The thoroughbred is used for pleasure riding.
   The standard breed is also used for pleasure riding.
   The quarter horse is used for pleasure riding, too.

   _____

   _____

   _____

3. Horses are used for riding.
   They are used for racing.
   They are used for ranch work.

   _____

   _____

   _____

4. The donkey is similar to a horse.
   The mule is similar to the horse.
   The zebra is similar to the horse.

   _____

   _____

   _____

5. The Morgan horse is known for its beauty.
   It is known for its good behavior.
   It is known for its endurance.

   _____

   _____

6. The quarter horse is used as a riding horse.
   It is used as a cattle horse.
   It is also used as a polo pony.

   _____

   _____

   _____

7. Draft horses include the Percheron.
   They include the Shire.
   They also include the Clydesdale.

   _____

   _____

   _____

8. Light horses are used for riding.
   They are used for racing.
   They are used for ranch work, too.

   _____

   _____

   _____

Writing/Writing Processes

Objective 4

Expectation: *edit drafts for specific purposes such as to ensure standard usage, varied sentence structure, and appropriate word choice*

DIRECTIONS: Find the sentence that best develops the topic sentence below.

1. **Our cat, Petunia, does the strangest thing.**

   (A) We got her two years ago from a friend. Since then, Petunia has become an important part of our family.

   (B) She is a gray cat with dark stripes. When I go to sleep at night, she loves to snuggle up beside me.

   (C) For no reason at all, she just starts running around the house. Then, without warning, Petunia finds a comfortable spot and falls sound asleep.

   (D) We also have a dog named Molly. Petunia and Molly get along well, and sometimes they eat out of the same bowl.

DIRECTIONS: Read each paragraph and find the sentence that does not belong.

2. **(1) The National Weather Service is a part of the United States government. (2) Another part of the government is the National Park Service. (3) The National Weather Service is responsible for preparing weather maps and making forecasts. (4) Many businesses and individuals depend on the National Weather Service to plan their activities.**

   (F) Sentence 1

   (G) Sentence 2

   (H) Sentence 3

   (J) Sentence 4

3. **(1) The water ouzel is a most remarkable bird. (2) Like many other birds, it feeds on insects. (3) Hummingbirds feed on nectar from flowers as well as insects. (4) But unlike other birds, the water ouzel often seeks its food by diving into a stream and walking along the bottom!**

   (A) Sentence 1

   (B) Sentence 2

   (C) Sentence 3

   (D) Sentence 4

DIRECTIONS: Read the paragraph. Then find the sentence that best fits in the blank.

4. **Rashad decided to join the ski club at his school. _____. Once a week, the ski club takes a bus to a ski area about two hours from school. Members are able to rent skis and buy a lift ticket for half-price.**

   (F) There were 12 other clubs at his school

   (G) He was a good student and enjoyed doing different things

   (H) His older sister had been in the history club at the same school

   (J) He had never skied before, but thought it looked like fun

STOP

Objective

4

Mini-Test

DIRECTIONS: Choose the answer that best combines the underlined sentences.

1. **Benjamin caught a fish.**
   The fish was large and had green stripes.

   (A) Benjamin caught a fish that had green stripes and was large.

   (B) Benjamin caught a fish that was large or had green stripes.

   (C) The fish was large that Benjamin caught and had green stripes.

   (D) Benjamin caught a large fish that had green stripes.

2. **The library had a book on the subject.**
   The book was old and dusty.

   (F) The library had an old, dusty book on the subject.

   (G) The book the library had on the subject was old, dusty.

   (H) The old and dusty book, the library had on the subject.

   (J) The library had a book on the subject and was old and dusty.

3. **Ju-Yong saw a whale.**
   The whale was blue.
   She saw it on her vacation.

   (A) Ju-Yong saw a whale on her vacation that was blue.

   (B) Ju-Yong saw a blue whale on her vacation.

   (C) The blue whale Ju-Yong saw on her vacation.

   (D) On her vacation Ju-Yong saw a whale and it was blue.

DIRECTIONS: Choose the answer that is a complete and correctly written sentence.

4. (F) The fire company responded quick to the call for help.

   (G) My family usually contributes to the fund drive for the fire company.

   (H) They were happily to see the ambulance.

   (J) Nicely people on the ambulance squad.

5. (A) Art class once a week with students in another class.

   (B) Entering a painting in the show.

   (C) Drawing and painting enjoyed by many young people.

   (D) The pot you made is beautiful.

DIRECTIONS: Read each sentence. Select the part of the sentence that is a prepositional phrase.

6. **The ice cream in the freezer is melting.**

   (F) The ice cream

   (G) ice cream in

   (H) in the freezer

   (J) is melting

7. **She tossed the ball over the fence.**

   (A) She tossed

   (B) the ball over

   (C) over the fence

   (D) tossed the ball

78

TAKS Writing—Objective 5

During editing and proofreading the competent writer should also review his or her text for the proper application of standard grammar and usage so that the writer communicates the message clearly. Incorrect use of tense, lack of agreement between subjects and verbs, and unclear pronoun referents can cause the reader to misunderstand the writer's meaning. Objective 5 tests the student's ability to recognize and correct errors in grammar and usage in the context of peer-editing passages.

The student will recognize standard usage and appropriate word choice in written text.

(4.18)   Writing/grammar/usage
The student applies standard grammar and usage to communicate clearly and effectively in writing. The student is expected to
- **(C)** employ standard English usage in writing for audiences, including subject-verb agreement, pronoun referents, and parts of speech (4–8); *(See page 80.)*
- **(D)** use adjectives (comparative and superlative forms) and adverbs appropriately to make writing vivid or precise (4–8); and *(See page 81.)*
- **(H)** write with increasing accuracy when using objective case pronouns such as "Dan cooked for you and me." (4–5). *(See page 82.)*

What it means:
- Comparative and superlative adjectives show things being compared. Comparative adjectives compare two things. Example: Ted is *taller* than Ken. She talks *more loudly* than Cara.
  Superlative adjectives are used to compare three or more things. Example: Of all the boys in the class, Ted is the *tallest*. She talks *most loudly*.
- Personal pronouns have three cases: nominative, objective, and possessive. Objective case pronouns serve as direct objects, indirect objects, or objects of prepositions. *Me, you, her, him, it, us, you,* and *them* are objective pronouns.

(4.19)   Writing/writing processes
The student selects and uses writing processes for self-initiated and assigned writing. The student is expected to
- **(E)** edit drafts for specific purposes such as to ensure standard usage, varied sentence structure, and appropriate word choice (4–8); and *(See page 83.)*
- **(H)** proofread his/her own writing and that of others (4–8). *(See page 84.)*

Writing/Grammar/Usage

Objective 5

Expectation: employ standard English usage in writing for audiences, including subject-verb agreement, pronoun referents, and parts of speech

---

DIRECTIONS: Choose the answer that completes the sentence best.

1. The gift _____ yesterday.

- (A) arrives
- (B) arrived
- (C) arriving
- (D) will arrive

2. Please _____ this letter to the post office.

- (F) took
- (G) has taken
- (H) had tooken
- (J) take

3. Jeff and Channa _____ us make bread.

- (A) had help
- (B) will help
- (C) helps
- (D) helping

4. No one _____ him about the change of plans.

- (F) telled
- (G) told
- (H) tells
- (J) did tell

DIRECTIONS: Choose the answer that uses an incorrect verb.

5.
- (A) The library have a room for music.
- (B) In the room, you can listen to tapes.
- (C) The room has lots of books about music.
- (D) I love spending time there.

6.
- (F) Chang has picked up her heavy backpack.
- (G) She carry that backpack everywhere.
- (H) It has all her art supplies in it.
- (J) She also carries her laptop in the backpack.

7.
- (A) He forgot to take his jacket home.
- (B) It was a cold day.
- (C) He shiver without his jacket.
- (D) He was very glad to get home at last.

8.
- (F) Nobody is home today.
- (G) The house are locked up.
- (H) It looks strange with the shades down.
- (J) I am not used to seeing it so empty.

80

Writing/Grammar/Usage

Objective 5

Expectation: *uses adjectives (comparative and superlative forms) and adverbs appropriately to make writing vivid or precise*

DIRECTIONS: Write whether the word in bold type is an *adjective* or an *adverb*.

1. **both** puppies _____

2. **blue** sky _____

3. ran **quickly** _____

4. **bad** report _____

5. finish **easily** _____

6. **soft** blanket _____

7. **often** help _____

8. **green** grass _____

9. **large** house _____

10. **black** clouds _____

11. **sweet** oranges _____

12. **sticky** glue _____

13. flew **high** _____

14. swam **yesterday** _____

15. **yellow** daisy _____

16. **broken** dish _____

17. ended **suddenly** _____

18. blew **strongly** _____

DIRECTIONS: Write a paragraph describing your favorite place in the world. Circle each adjective and adverb you use in your description.

19. _____

_____

_____

_____

_____

_____

_____

_____

_____

_____

_____

_____

_____

_____

_____

_____

_____

_____

_____

_____

_____

STOP

Writing/Grammar/Usage

**Objective
5**

Expectation: write with increasing accuracy when using objective case pronouns such as "Dan cooked for you and me."

DIRECTIONS: Replace the underlined word or words with a pronoun.

1. Terry said she would follow <u>the team</u> in her van.

   _____

2. I have not seen <u>your parents</u> this weekend.

   _____

3. Have you met <u>Joshua</u>?

   _____

4. Tell <u>Katrina</u> we are sorry we missed the show.

   _____

5. I've lost <u>my ring</u> down the sink!

   _____

6. The Whites said they'd meet <u>my parents</u> and me in the parking lot.

   _____

7. We asked <u>the Taylors</u> to bring extra folding chairs.

   _____

8. You will sit next to Misha and <u>Judith</u>.

   _____

9. <u>The skateboard</u> is all waxed and ready to go.

   _____

10. I have seen <u>the movie</u> already.

    _____

11. Did you remember to bring the ice for <u>the girls and me</u>?

    _____

12. Can you tell me where <u>the new restaurant</u> will be built?

    _____

13. Let's make some cookies for <u>our new neighbors</u>.

    _____

14. That is <u>Cody's</u> glove in the outfield.

    _____

15. <u>Florida</u> is my favorite place to go for vacation.

    _____

Writing/Writing Processes

Objective 5

Expectation: *edit drafts for specific purposes such as to ensure standard usage, varied sentence structure, and appropriate word choice*

DIRECTIONS: Fill in the blanks with the correct form of *there*, *their*, or *they're*.

1. **Nancy and Sue are feeding**

   _____ **pets.**

2. _____ **feeding the ducks, rabbits, and geese first.**

3. **"Nancy, would you carry this bag of food**

   over _____ **?" asked Sue.**

4. **"I will carry it over** _____ **if you will watch that the rabbits don't run**

   out of _____ **cage," said Sue.**

5. **"**_____ **gone!" shouted Nancy.**

6. **The girls looked and saw** _____ **pet rabbits running off behind the bushes.**

7. **"**_____ **they are!" exclaimed Sue.**

8. **Nancy and Sue caught** _____ **rabbits and put them**

   in _____ **cage.**

9. _____ **now going into the house to feed**

   _____ **fish.**

10. **"At least the fish can't swim out**

    of _____ **aquarium!" exclaimed Nancy.**

DIRECTIONS: Choose the best way of expressing the idea.

11. Ⓐ Toward San Francisco a group of pioneers thought they were headed.

    Ⓑ San Francisco, they thought the pioneers were headed.

    Ⓒ A group of pioneers thought they were headed toward San Francisco.

    Ⓓ A group of pioneers toward San Francisco were headed.

12. Ⓕ Lost City was soon known for its fine seafood.

    Ⓖ Soon, Lost City was known for its fine seafood.

    Ⓗ For its fine seafood, Lost City was known soon.

    Ⓙ Lost City, for its fine seafood, was soon known.

STOP

Writing/Writing Processes

Objective
5

Expectation: *proofread his/her own writing and that of others*

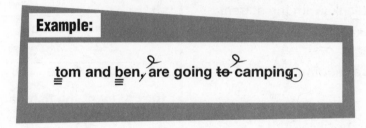

Example:

tom and ben, are going to camping.

DIRECTIONS: Use proofreader's marks to correct the punctuation in the report below.

Did you know that bats are mammals mother bats nurse baby bats when they

are young. when the young bats get to be two or three weeks old, they start to find

food for themselves

Has anyone ever told you you're "blind as a bat" when you can't find something

if someone tells you this, you can tell them that bats are not blind? They have good eyes

and a good sense of smell. bats. are unusual, however, because they bounce sound waves

off objects to help them know where they are. This! is called *echolocation*

if you're lucky, you may see a bat Bats roost in hollow trees, crevices in rocks,

and caves They come out at twilight or at night to look for food What do you think a

bat's idea of a delicious! meal is Well, most of them feed on insects, but some eat

fruit, nectar, and pollen very few dine on small animals

STOP

Objective

5

Mini-Test

DIRECTIONS: Read the paragraph and answer the questions.

(1) "Boy, does this sound like a goofy assignment," I said to Kendra, rolling my eyes. (2) We were walking home after school talking about what Mr. Stewart had given her and I for homework this week.

(3) We was supposed to listen—just listen—for two hours this week. (4) We could do it any time we wanted, in short periods or long, and write down some of the stuffs we heard. (5) We also had to describe where we listened and the time of day.

(6) As we walked by a park, Kendra stopped for a moment and suggested, "Hey, I have an idea. Let us start right now."

(7) For once her had something. (8) I told her it was a great idea, then spotted an bench beside the fountain. (9) "Let's get started," I said.

1. In sentence 1, *rolling* is best written —

- (A) rollering
- (B) rolleded
- (C) rolled
- (D) As it is

2. In sentence 2, *her and I* is best written —

- (F) us
- (G) we students
- (H) she and myself
- (J) As it is

3. In sentence 3, *we was* is best written —

- (A) we are
- (B) we am
- (C) we were
- (D) As it is

4. In sentence 4, *the stuffs* is best written —

- (F) the stuff
- (G) a stuffs
- (H) an stuff
- (J) As it is

5. In sentence 6, *Let us* is best written —

- (A) Lets
- (B) Lets us
- (C) Let's
- (D) As it is

6. In sentence 7, *her had* is best written —

- (F) her have
- (G) she have
- (H) her has
- (J) she had

7. In sentence 8, *an bench* is best written —

- (A) an benches
- (B) a bench
- (C) a benches
- (D) As it is

STOP

TAKS Writing—Objective 6

Effective writers examine their work for correct capitalization, punctuation, and spelling.

Capitalization and punctuation marks take the place of the pauses, stops, and intonations used to convey meaning in oral communication. Accuracy in mechanics helps the reader "hear" those nuances and better understand what the writer is trying to communicate. Correct spelling is also necessary for accurate meaning. Objective 6 tests the student's ability to recognize and correct errors in capitalization, punctuation, and spelling in the context of peer-editing passages.

The student will proofread for correct punctuation, capitalization, and spelling in written text.

(4.16)   Writing/penmanship/capitalization/punctuation
The student composes original texts, applying the conventions of written language such as capitalization, punctuation, and penmanship to communicate clearly. The student is expected to

- **(B)** capitalize and punctuate correctly to clarify and enhance meaning such as capitalizing titles, using possessives, commas in a series, commas in direct address, and sentence punctuation (4–5). (*See page 87.*)

(4.17)   Writing/spelling
The student spells proficiently. The student is expected to

- **(A)** write with accurate spelling of syllable constructions, including closed, open, consonant before –le, and syllable boundary patterns (3–6); (*See page 88.*)
- **(B)** write with accurate spelling of roots such as drink, speak, read, or happy, inflections such as those that change tense or number, suffixes such as –able or –less, and prefixes such as re– or un– (4–6); and (*See page 89.*)
- **(D)** spell accurately in final drafts (4–8). (*See page 90.*)

(4.18)   Writing/grammar/usage
The student applies standard grammar and usage to communicate clearly and effectively in writing. The student is expected to

- **(G)** write with increasing accuracy when using apostrophes in contractions such as it's and possessives such as Jan's (4 –8). (*See page 91.*)

(4.19)   Writing/writing processes
The student selects and uses writing processes for self- initiated and assigned writing. The student is expected to

- **(H)** proofread his/her own writing and that of others (4–8). (*See page 92.*)

Writing/Penmanship/Capitalization/Punctuation

Objective 6

Expectation: *capitalize and punctuate correctly to clarify and enhance meaning such as capitalizing titles, using possessives, commas in a series, commas in direct address, and sentence punctuation*

DIRECTIONS: Decide which punctuation mark, if any, is needed in the underlined part of each sentence.

1. **The puppy couldn't find the food <u>dish</u>**
   - (A) ,
   - (B) .
   - (C) ?
   - (D) None

2. **"This is <u>fun,</u> answered Lettie.**
   - (F) ,
   - (G) ?
   - (H) "
   - (J) None

3. **<u>Jeff</u> will you please bring in the newspaper?**
   - (A) !
   - (B) ,
   - (C) ?
   - (D) None

4. **<u>Lisas</u> brother is studying to be a dentist.**
   - (F) .
   - (G) 's
   - (H) '
   - (J) None

DIRECTIONS: Choose the answer that is written correctly and shows the correct capitalization and punctuation.

5.
   - (A) The Tennis courts are full
   - (B) Venus put our names on the list.
   - (C) Did you remember your racket.
   - (D) This can of Tennis balls is new?

6.
   - (F) Tell Mrs Jensen I called.
   - (G) Miss. Richards will be late.
   - (H) Our coach is Mr Wanamaker.
   - (J) Dr. Cullinane was here earlier.

7. **Winters are warm in <u>Tucson Arizona</u>.**
   - (A) Tucson, arizona
   - (B) Tucson Arizona,
   - (C) Tucson, Arizona.
   - (D) Correct as is

8. **The play will be held on Wednesday, <u>Thursday, and Friday,</u> nights.**
   - (F) Thursday, and Friday
   - (G) Thursday, and, Friday
   - (H) Thursday and Friday,
   - (J) Correct as is

STOP

Writing/Spelling

Objective
6

Expectation: *write with accurate spelling of syllable constructions, including closed, open, consonant before –le, and syllable boundary patterns*

DIRECTIONS: Divide the underlined word in each sentence into syllables.

1. Ben earned his <u>patch</u> for camping.

   _____

2. "It is <u>possible</u> that we could be in lost," he said.

   _____

3. We used the last of the water in our canteens to <u>pour</u> on the fire.

   _____

4. Some of the other scouts will <u>remain</u> in the lodge.

   _____

5. The <u>royal</u> coach will pick up the princess at the steps.

   _____

6. We were so tired, we <u>slept</u> until noon.

   _____

7. The name of the publisher should be under the book's <u>title</u>.

   _____

8. Ariel lit the <u>torch</u> before entering the cave.

   _____

9. Charlie was our pet <u>turtle</u>.

   _____

10. Only the magic key will <u>unlock</u> the golden door.

    _____

11. Mr. Warner's <u>vegetable</u> garden looks very healthy.

    _____

12. We fed the <u>whole</u> loaf of bread to the ducks.

    _____

13. We heard the <u>wild</u> turkeys in the woods behind the cabin.

    _____

14. There is a great story in every <u>issue</u> of this magazine.

    _____

15. Tina is going to the <u>lecture</u> about model trains.

    _____

16. Warren likes to visit the horses in the <u>stable</u>.

    _____

Writing/Spelling

Objective 6

Expectation: write with accurate spelling of roots such as drink, speak, read, or happy, inflections such as those that change tense or number, suffixes such as –able or –less, and prefixes such as re– or un–

DIRECTIONS: Choose a word to fill the blank that fits the meaning of the words in parentheses.

1. The water was so bitter it was (not able to be drunk).

   _____

2. Jan asked us to (read again) Chapter 6.

   _____

3. When Jess learned he did not get the job he was very (not happy).

   _____

4. Mel was (not able to speak) when we gave him the gift.

   _____

5. The little boat was (not able to be sunk) in the storm.

   _____

DIRECTIONS: Choose the correct definition for the root in each word.

6. In the word *abbreviate*, *brev* means
   - Ⓐ to lengthen
   - Ⓑ to shorten
   - Ⓒ to make a list
   - Ⓓ to learn how to spell

7. In the word *autograph*, *graph* means
   - Ⓕ to read
   - Ⓖ to draw a picture
   - Ⓗ to write
   - Ⓙ to measure something

8. In the word *telescope*, *tele* means
   - Ⓐ empty space
   - Ⓑ far away
   - Ⓒ close up
   - Ⓓ temperature

9. In the word *geography*, *geo* means
   - Ⓕ stars
   - Ⓖ Earth
   - Ⓗ the human body
   - Ⓙ insects

10. In the word *triangle*, *tri* means
    - Ⓐ one
    - Ⓑ two
    - Ⓒ three
    - Ⓓ four

11. In the word *bicycle*, *cycl* means
    - Ⓕ wheel
    - Ⓖ handlebars
    - Ⓗ spokes
    - Ⓙ chain

12. In the word *action*, *ac* means
    - Ⓐ eat
    - Ⓑ fill
    - Ⓒ subtract
    - Ⓓ do

13. In the word *autobiography*, *auto* means
    - Ⓕ car
    - Ⓖ friendly
    - Ⓗ self
    - Ⓙ television

STOP

Name _____ Date _____

Writing/Spelling

Objective
6

Expectation: *spell accurately in final drafts*

DIRECTIONS: Find the word that is spelled correctly and fits best in the blank.

1. **Please _____ your work.**
   - (A) revew
   - (B) reeview
   - (C) review
   - (D) raview

2. **He is my best _____ .**
   - (F) frind
   - (G) frend
   - (H) friend
   - (J) freind

3. **We can _____ the gymnasium.**
   - (A) decarate
   - (B) decorait
   - (C) decorrate
   - (D) decorate

4. **The store is in a good _____ .**
   - (F) locashun
   - (G) locashin
   - (H) locatin
   - (J) location

5. **Students were _____ for bravery.**
   - (A) honored
   - (B) honord
   - (C) honered
   - (D) honard

6. **We need a new _____ .**
   - (F) vidio recorder
   - (G) video recorder
   - (H) video recordor
   - (J) vidio ricorder

7. **This _____ leads to the gym.**
   - (A) stareway
   - (B) stareweigh
   - (C) stairweigh
   - (D) stairway

8. **Three _____ people lived in the city.**
   - (F) milion
   - (G) millun
   - (H) millione
   - (J) million

9. **Did you finish the _____ yet?**
   - (A) lesson
   - (B) leson
   - (C) lessin
   - (D) lessan

10. **We planted _____ along the fence.**
    - (F) daisyes
    - (G) daisies
    - (H) daisys
    - (J) daises

Writing/Grammar/Usage

Objective 6

Expectation: *write with increasing accuracy when using apostrophes in contractions such as it's and possessives such as Jan's*

DIRECTIONS: Choose either *its* or *it's* for each sentence below.

1. _____ snowing!

2. _____ about time I learn how to do this.

3. After dinner, the cat licked _____ paws.

4. _____ late so I had better be going.

5. The horse shook _____ long mane.

6. Surprise! _____ your birthday.

7. That car has lost half _____ fender.

8. _____ my favorite book.

9. I can't wait until _____ Valentine's Day.

10. _____ mane was braided.

DIRECTIONS: Choose the word or words that best fit in the blank and have correct punctuation.

11. My _____ car is in the garage.
    - (A) sister
    - (B) sister's
    - (C) sisters'
    - (D) sisters

12. Which of these tennis rackets is _____?
    - (F) your's
    - (G) yours
    - (H) youres
    - (J) you'res

13. My _____ were born in El Paso.
    - (A) friends parents
    - (B) friend's parents
    - (C) friends parent's
    - (D) friends parents'

14. That was the best movie _____ ever seen.
    - (F) I've
    - (G) Ive
    - (H) Iv'e
    - (J) Ive'

15. You wouldn't believe how funny _____ costume is.
    - (A) Tammys
    - (B) Tammys'
    - (C) Tamm'ys
    - (D) Tammy's

16. The coach said we _____ get trophies this year.
    - (F) willn't
    - (G) won't
    - (H) wo'nt
    - (J) wont

STOP

Writing/Writing Processes

Objective 6

Expectation: proofread his/her own writing and that of others

---

DIRECTIONS: Rachel has written an article about the Junior Red Cross's clothing drive. The article will appear in the school newspaper. Help Rachel proofread her work using proofreader's marks.

Lets all get together and help the Junior Red Cross. There are

lotss of people needing the organizations help right now. Theyre

sponsoring a clothing drive to help people caught inn the recent

flood. Womens dresses, mens shirts, and childrens clothing are

especially nneeded. If youve outgrown any clothing or have clothing

you dont use, please bring it in. Itll help brighten someones day!

DIRECTIONS: Rewrite the article correctly on the lines below.

_____

_____

_____

_____

_____

_____

_____

_____

_____

_____

_____

_____

Objective

6

Mini-Test

DIRECTIONS: Choose the sentence that is written correctly and shows the correct capitalization and punctuation.

1. (A) Suzie whispered, "This is a great movie."

   (B) "Don't forget your money said Mother."

   (C) Are there seats up front?" asked Bruce?

   (D) "Let's get popcorn" suggested Wanda.

2. (F) Dad bought seeds plants, and fertilizer.

   (G) The shovel rake and hoe are in the garage.

   (H) We usually camp with Jan, Bob and, Annie.

   (J) The garden had corn, beans, and peas.

DIRECTIONS: Look at the underlined part of the paragraph. Choose the answer that shows the best capitalization and punctuation for that part.

(3) Ricky said, "Watch what I can do." He rode his **(4)** bike to the middle of the driveway. And balanced himself **(5)** on the back wheel. Il'l bet there isn't another kid in **(6)** mayfield who can do that.

3. (A) said, Watch

   (B) said, "watch

   (C) said "Watch

   (D) Correct as it is

4. (F) driveway and

   (G) driveway and,

   (H) driveway And

   (J) Correct as it is

5. (A) Ill bet

   (B) Ill' bet

   (C) I'll bet

   (D) Correct as it is

6. (F) mayfield. Who

   (G) Mayfield who

   (H) mayfield, who

   (J) Correct as it is

DIRECTIONS: Choose the phrase in which the underlined word is not spelled correctly.

7. (A) quick reply

   (B) feel helples

   (C) important news

   (D) living well

8. (F) patch a tire

   (G) pancake batter

   (H) wipe a dish

   (J) leave earley

9. (A) win a prize

   (B) group meeting

   (C) comfortabel chair

   (D) repair a tire

STOP

How Am I Doing?

Objective 1 Mini-Test Page 51 **Number Correct**	**4** answers correct	**Great Job!** Move on to the section test on page 96.
	3 answers correct	**You're almost there!** But you still need a little practice. Review practice pages 45–50 before moving on to the section test on page 96.
	0–2 answers correct	**Oops!** Time to review what you have learned and try again. Review the practice section on pages 45–50. Then retake the test on page 51. Now move on to the section test on page 96.
Objective 2 Mini-Test Page 68 **Number Correct**	**9–10** answers correct	**Awesome!** Move on to the section test on page 96.
	6–8 answers correct	**You're almost there!** But you still need a little practice. Review practice pages 53–67 before moving on to the section test on page 96.
	0–5 answers correct	**Oops!** Time to review what you have learned and try again. Review the practice section on pages 53–67. Then retake the test on page 68. Now move on to the section test on page 96.
Objective 3 Mini-Test Page 72 **Number Correct**	**4** answers correct	**Great Job!** Move on to the section test on page 96.
	3 answers correct	**You're almost there!** But you still need a little practice. Review practice pages 70–71 before moving on to the section test on page 96.
	0–2 answers correct	**Oops!** Time to review what you have learned and try again. Review the practice section on pages 70–71. Then retake the test on page 72. Now move on to the section test on page 96.

How Am I Doing?

Objective 4 Mini-Test	7 answers correct	**Great Job!** Move on to the section test on page 96.
Page 78 **Number Correct**	5–6 answers correct	**You're almost there!** But you still need a little practice. Review practice pages 74–77 before moving on to the section test on page 96.
	0–4 answers correct	**Oops!** Time to review what you have learned and try again. Review the practice section on pages 74–77. Then retake the test on page 78. Now move on to the section test on page 96.
Objective 5 Mini-Test	7 answers correct	**Awesome!** Move on to the section test on page 96.
Page 85 **Number Correct**	5–6 answers correct	**You're almost there!** But you still need a little practice. Review practice pages 80–84 before moving on to the section test on page 96.
	0–4 answers correct	**Oops!** Time to review what you have learned and try again. Review the practice section on pages 80–84. Then retake the test on page 85. Now move on to the section test on page 96.
Objective 6 Mini-Test	8–9 answers correct	**Great Job!** Move on to the section test on page 96.
Page 93 **Number Correct**	5–7 answers correct	**You're almost there!** But you still need a little practice. Review practice pages 87–92 before moving on to the section test on page 96.
	0–4 answers correct	**Oops!** Time to review what you have learned and try again. Review the practice section on pages 87–92. Then retake the test on page 93. Now move on to the section test on page 96.

Name _____   Date _____

Final Test for
Writing
for pages 45–93

DIRECTIONS: Choose the line that has a punctuation error. If there is no error, choose "No mistakes."

1. (A) The bus will pick us up
    (B) at 830 A.M. sharp for
    (C) the field trip to the zoo.
    (D) No mistakes

2. (F) Sara wanted to adopt
    (G) another greyhound but
    (H) she simply didn't have room.
    (J) No mistakes

DIRECTIONS: Choose the word or words that fit best in the blank and shows correct punctuation.

3. _____ we won't be seeing that film.
    (A) No
    (B) No,
    (C) No;
    (D) No:

4. _____ and Russ all went to get their hair cut.
    (F) Max Mikey
    (G) Max, Mikey,
    (H) Max Mikey,
    (J) Max Mikey;

5. **Teresa yelled, _____ .**
    (A) come back!
    (B) "come back!"
    (C) "Come Back!"
    (D) "Come back!"

DIRECTIONS: Choose the answer that shows the best way to write the underlined part.

(1) Can you imagine finding a bottle with a message inside—or perhaps one containing <u>money</u>? **(2)** <u>bottles</u> may travel thousands of miles in the ocean. **(3)** Not long ago a child in <u>new york</u> found a bottle that had been washed up on the beach. **(4)** Inside was <u>1,700</u>! **(5)** After waiting a year, the youngster was allowed to keep the money.

6. **In sentence 1, *money?* is best written —**
    (F) money!
    (G) money.
    (H) Money?
    (J) As it is

7. **In sentence 2, *bottles* is best written —**
    (A) Bottles;
    (B) Bottles,
    (C) Bottles
    (D) As it is

8. **In sentence 3, *new york* is best written —**
    (F) New York
    (G) New York,
    (H) New york
    (J) As it is

9. **In sentence 4, *1,700!* is best written —**
    (A) 1700.
    (B) $1,700!
    (C) $1,700?
    (D) As it is

Name _____ Date _____

DIRECTIONS: Read each sentence. Choose the underlined part that is misspelled. If all words are spelled correctly, choose "No mistake."

10. We <u>should</u> <u>probly</u> go inside before the <u>thunderstorm</u> starts. <u>No mistake</u>
    (F)   (G)   (H)   (J)

11. Our dog <u>always</u> <u>houls</u> at the moon on <u>Thursday</u> nights. <u>No mistake</u>
    (A)   (B)   (C)   (D)

12. The <u>weather</u> <u>forecast</u> for this weekend looks <u>postitive</u>. <u>No mistake</u>
    (F)   (G)   (H)   (J)

13. Sharon was <u>completing</u> a <u>puzzle</u> with her <u>classmate</u> Marty. <u>No mistake</u>
    (A)   (B)   (C)   (D)

DIRECTIONS: Read each answer. Choose the answer that has an error. If none have an error, choose "No mistakes."

14.
(F) our car
(G) they're dog
(H) his bank
(J) No mistakes

15.
(A) Gina and I share a locker.
(B) It's for Gina and I.
(C) It's for Gina and me.
(D) No mistakes

16.
(F) He and I are tired.
(G) We crossed the Ohio River.
(H) I read The Fall Of the Empire.
(J) No mistakes

17.
(A) Its batteries are dead.
(B) Jonah's swing
(C) Magic Maxes' trick
(D) No mistakes

18.
(F) We students were ready to go.
(G) Us students were tired of walking
(H) Our parents were to meet us at the bus.
(J) No mistakes

GO

DIRECTIONS: Choose the word that is spelled correctly and fits best in the blank.

19. Jerrod made a wise _____.
- Ⓐ dicision
- Ⓑ decision
- Ⓒ decison
- Ⓓ decesion

20. We had a special meeting _____ night.
- Ⓕ Wenesday
- Ⓖ Wensday
- Ⓗ Wendsday
- Ⓙ Wednesday

21. The firefighters made a daring _____.
- Ⓐ rescew
- Ⓑ reskue
- Ⓒ rescu
- Ⓓ rescue

22. There was a _____ accident on the highway.
- Ⓕ terrible
- Ⓖ terruble
- Ⓗ terible
- Ⓙ terrable

23. Would you please _____ the dial on the radio?
- Ⓐ ajust
- Ⓑ adjust
- Ⓒ adjussed
- Ⓓ edjust

24. Do you want a _____ of cake?
- Ⓕ piece
- Ⓖ peace
- Ⓗ peice
- Ⓙ pice

DIRECTIONS: Choose the line that has a usage error. If there is no error, choose "No mistakes."

25.
- Ⓐ Me and Paige want to
- Ⓑ go horseback riding this
- Ⓒ Saturday if the weather is good.
- Ⓓ No mistakes

26.
- Ⓕ It wasn't no bother to
- Ⓖ retype that paper since
- Ⓗ I had to do mine too.
- Ⓙ No mistakes

27.
- Ⓐ Please clean up the dinner
- Ⓑ dishes before you start
- Ⓒ watching television.
- Ⓓ No mistakes

DIRECTIONS: Choose the answer that fits best in the blank and shows correct capitalization and punctuation.

28. _____ for the cool camera.
- Ⓕ Thank you,
- Ⓖ thank you
- Ⓗ Thank, you
- Ⓙ Thank you

29. The play will be held on Wednesday, _____ nights.
- Ⓐ Thursday, and Friday,
- Ⓑ Thursday, and, Friday
- Ⓒ Thursday, and Friday
- Ⓓ Thursday and Friday,

30. Our project is due on _____.

- (F) October 28 2002
- (G) October 28, 2002
- (H) October 28 2002
- (J) October, 28, 2002

31. Please send that to _____.

- (A) Mankato, Minnesota
- (B) mankato Minnesota
- (C) mankato minnesota
- (D) mankato, Minnesota,

DIRECTIONS: Choose the answer that best combines the underlined sentences.

32. The driver put the turn signal on. The driver turned right.

- (F) The driver turned right but put the turn signal on.
- (G) The driver put the turn signal on and turned right.
- (H) Turning right, the driver putting the turn signal on.
- (J) The driver, who put the turn signal on, and turned right.

33. The room was filled with children. The children were happy.

- (A) The room was filled with happy children.
- (B) The room was filled and the children were happy.
- (C) The children were happy who filled the room.
- (D) Filled with happy children was the room.

34. The mall is new. The mall is near my house. The mall is very large.

- (F) Near my house is a mall and it is very large and new.
- (G) Large and new, the mall is near my house.
- (H) The mall near my house is new, and the mall is very large.
- (J) The new mall near my house is very large.

DIRECTIONS: Choose the best way of expressing the idea.

35.
- (A) Please help me put out the trash, but before you go to school.
- (B) Please help me before you go to school put out the trash.
- (C) Help me before you go to school the trash to put out.
- (D) Before you go to school, please help me put out the trash.

36.
- (F) At our school swims my sister on the team.
- (G) The team at our school on which my sister swims.
- (H) My sister swims on the team at our school.
- (J) My sister at our school swims on the team.

STOP

Name _____ Date _____

Writing Test
Answer Sheet

1 (A) (B) (C) (D)
2 (F) (G) (H) (J)
3 (A) (B) (C) (D)
4 (F) (G) (H) (J)
5 (A) (B) (C) (D)
6 (F) (G) (H) (J)
7 (A) (B) (C) (D)
8 (F) (G) (H) (J)
9 (A) (B) (C) (D)
10 (F) (G) (H) (J)

11 (A) (B) (C) (D)
12 (F) (G) (H) (J)
13 (A) (B) (C) (D)
14 (F) (G) (H) (J)
15 (A) (B) (C) (D)
16 (F) (G) (H) (J)
17 (A) (B) (C) (D)
18 (F) (G) (H) (J)
19 (A) (B) (C) (D)
20 (F) (G) (H) (J)

21 (A) (B) (C) (D)
22 (F) (G) (H) (J)
23 (A) (B) (C) (D)
24 (F) (G) (H) (J)
25 (A) (B) (C) (D)
26 (F) (G) (H) (J)
27 (A) (B) (C) (D)
28 (F) (G) (H) (J)
29 (A) (B) (C) (D)
30 (F) (G) (H) (J)

31 (A) (B) (C) (D)
32 (F) (G) (H) (J)
33 (A) (B) (C) (D)
34 (F) (G) (H) (J)
35 (A) (B) (C) (D)
36 (F) (G) (H) (J)

Mathematics
Content Standards

The mathematics section of the state test measures knowledge in six different areas.

1) Objective 1: Number, operation, and quantitative reasoning

2) Objective 2: Patterns, relationships, and algebraic thinking

3) Objective 3: Geometry and spatial reasoning

4) Objective 4: Measurement

5) Objective 5: Probability and Statistics

6) Objective 6: Underlying processes and mathematical tools

Mathematics
Table of Contents

Mathematics Chart
Grade 4

Length

Metric

1 kilometer = 1000 meters

1 meter = 100 centimeters

1 centimeter = 10 millimeters

Customary

1 mile = 1760 yards

1 mile = 5280 feet

1 yard = 3 feet

1 foot = 12 inches

Time

1 year = 365 days

1 year = 12 months

1 year = 52 weeks

1 week = 7 days

1 day = 24 hours

1 hour = 60 minutes

1 minute = 60 seconds

Capacity and Volume

Metric

1 liter = 1000 milliliters

Customary

1 gallon = 4 quarts

1 gallon = 128 ounces

1 quart = 2 pints

1 pint = 2 cups

1 cup = 8 ounces

Mass and Weight

Metric

1 kilogram = 1000 grams

1 gram = 1000 milligrams

Customary

1 ton = 2000 pounds

1 pound = 16 ounces

Perimeter

square $\qquad$ $P = 4s$

rectangle $\qquad$ $P = 2\ell + 2w$ **or** $P = 2(\ell + w)$

Area

rectangle $\qquad$ $A = \ell w$ or $A = bh$

Centimeters

Inches

TAKS Mathematics—Objective 1

The student will demonstrate an understanding of numbers, operations, and quantitative reasoning.

(4.1) Number, operation, and quantitative reasoning
The student uses place value to represent whole numbers and decimals. The student is expected to
- **(A)** use place value to read, write, compare, and order whole numbers through the millions place. *(See page 104.)*

(4.2) Number, operation, and quantitative reasoning
The student describes and compares fractional parts of whole objects or sets of objects. The student is expected to
- **(A)** generate equivalent fractions using [concrete and] pictorial models; *(See page 105.)*
- **(B)** model fraction quantities greater than one using [concrete materials and] pictures; *(See page 106.)*
- **(C)** compare and order fractions using [concrete and] pictorial models; and *(See pages 107–108.)*
- **(D)** relate decimals to fractions that name tenths and hundredths using models. *(See page 109.)*

(4.3) Number, operation, and quantitative reasoning
The student adds and subtracts to solve meaningful problems involving whole numbers and decimals. The student is expected to
- **(A)** use addition and subtraction to solve problems involving whole numbers; and *(See pages 110–111.)*
- **(B)** add and subtract decimals to the hundredths place using [concrete and] pictorial models. *(See page 112.)*

(4.4) Number, operation, and quantitative reasoning
The student multiplies and divides to solve meaningful problems involving whole numbers. The student is expected to
- **(A)** model factors and products using arrays and area models; *(See page 113.)*

What it means:
- An array is an arrangement of items in a number of equal-sized rows. For example, an array of cans could be four rows of six, which shows that $4 \times 6 = 24$.
- Area models would show that length (l) $\times$ width (w) = area (A). For example, a carpet that is 4 feet by 6 feet has an area of 24 square feet.

- **(B)** represent multiplication and division situations in picture, word, and number form; *(See page 114.)*
- **(C)** recall and apply multiplication facts through 12×12; *(See page 115.)*
- **(D)** use multiplication to solve problems involving two-digit numbers; *(See page 116.)*
- **(E)** use division to solve problems involving one-digit divisors. *(See page 117.)*

(4.5) Number, operation, and quantitative reasoning
The student estimates to determine reasonable results. The student is expected to
- **(A)** round whole numbers to the nearest ten, hundred, or thousand to approximate reasonable results in problem situations; and *(See page 118.)*
- **(B)** estimate a product or quotient beyond basic facts. *(See page 119.)*

Number, Operation, and Quantitative Reasoning

Objective
1

Expectation: use place value to read, write, compare, and order whole numbers through the millions place

---

DIRECTIONS: Choose the best answer.

1. What is the numeral for twenty five million, three hundred fifty two thousand, twenty one?

- (A) 2,535,221
- (B) 25,352,210
- (C) 250,352,021
- (D) 25,352,021

2. What is the word name for 100,382,004?

- (F) one hundred million, three hundred eighty two thousand, four
- (G) one million, three hundred eighty two thousand, four hundred
- (H) one hundred million, three hundred eighty two thousand, four hundred
- (J) one million, three hundred eighty two thousand, four

3. What is the numeral for three million, twenty eight thousand, fourteen?

- (A) 3,028,014
- (B) 3,280,014
- (C) 3,028,140
- (D) 3,208,140

4. What is the word name for 352,000,001?

- (F) three hundred fifty two million, hundred thousand, one
- (G) three hundred fifty two million, one hundred
- (H) three hundred fifty two million, hundred thousand
- (J) three hundred fifty two million, one

5. What is the word name for 8,437,291?

- (A) eight thousand, four hundred thirty seven thousand, two hundred ninety one
- (B) eight million, four hundred thirty seven thousand, two hundred ninety one
- (C) eight hundred thousand, four hundred thirty seven thousand, two hundred ninety one
- (D) eight million, four hundred thirty thousand, two hundred ninety one

6. Which number is between 456,789 and 562,325?

- (F) 572,325
- (G) 564,331
- (H) 455,644
- (J) 458,319

7. If these numbers are put in order from greatest to least, what is the number exactly in the middle?

45 55 50 65 30 35 75

- (A) 45
- (B) 50
- (C) 35
- (D) 30

STOP

Name _____   Date _____

Number, Operation, and Quantitative Reasoning

Objective 1

Expectation: *generate equivalent fractions using pictorial models*

Example:

Which number does not show how much of the figure is shaded?

Ⓐ $\frac{1}{2}$ Ⓑ $\frac{5}{10}$

Ⓒ $\frac{1}{3}$ Ⓓ $\frac{10}{20}$

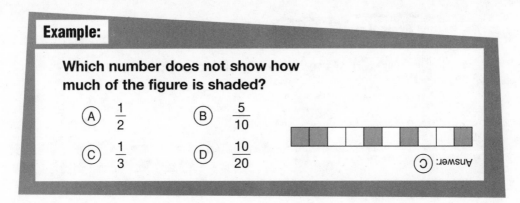

Answer: C

DIRECTIONS: Choose the best answer.

1. Which of the following is equivalent to $\frac{2}{6}$?

   Ⓐ

   Ⓑ

   Ⓒ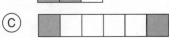

   Ⓓ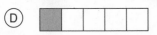

2. Which of the following fractions does not represent the portion of figures that are shaded?

   Ⓕ $\frac{1}{2}$

   Ⓖ $\frac{6}{12}$

   Ⓗ $\frac{7}{9}$

   Ⓙ $\frac{4}{8}$

3. What picture shows a fraction equivalent to $\frac{3}{10}$?

   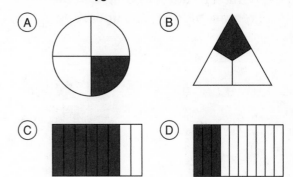

4. What fraction of this shape is shaded?

   Ⓕ $\frac{1}{2}$

   Ⓖ $\frac{3}{11}$

   Ⓗ $\frac{1}{3}$

   Ⓙ $\frac{2}{3}$

STOP

Number, Operation, and Quantitative Reasoning

Objective
1

Expectation: *model fraction quantities greater than one using pictures*

Example:

Which of the following pictures represents $1\frac{1}{2}$?

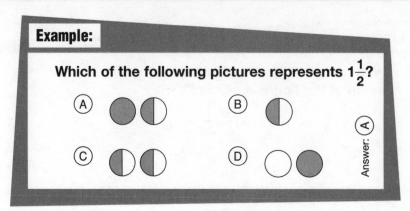

Answer: (A)

DIRECTIONS: Choose the best answer.

1. **Which of the following can be represented by this figure?**

   (A) $\frac{3}{4}$

   (B) $3\frac{3}{4}$

   (C) $3\frac{1}{3}$

   (D) $\frac{3}{13}$

2. **Which of the following represents 1?**

   (F)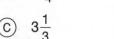

   (G) ★★☆☆

   (H) ★★★★

   (J) ★★☆☆

3. **Which of the following represents $2\frac{1}{4}$?**

   (A)

   (B)

   (C)

   (D)

4. **Which of the following can be represented by this figure?**

   (F) $4\frac{5}{6}$

   (G) $4\frac{2}{5}$

   (H) $4\frac{1}{5}$

   (J) $5\frac{1}{5}$

5. **Which of the following represents 0?**

   (A) ✦✦✦✦

   (B) ✦✦✦✦

   (C) ★✦✦✦

   (D) ✦✦✦✦

6. **Which of the following can be represented by this figure?**

   (F) $1\frac{5}{8}$

   (G) $\frac{5}{8}$

   (H) $1\frac{3}{8}$

   (J) $\frac{3}{8}$

STOP

Name _____ Date _____

Number, Operation, and Quantitative Reasoning

Objective
1

Expectation: compare and order fractions using pictorial models.

DIRECTIONS: Choose the best answer.

1. The scale to the right is balanced. All the figures with the same shape have the same weight. Which of the scales below is also balanced?

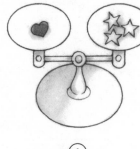  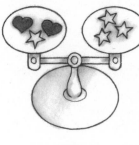 

Ⓐ   Ⓑ   Ⓒ   Ⓓ

2.

Ⓕ $\frac{2}{4} < \frac{3}{4}$

Ⓖ $\frac{2}{4} > \frac{3}{4}$

3.

Ⓐ $\frac{2}{3} < \frac{1}{3}$

Ⓑ $\frac{2}{3} > \frac{1}{3}$

4.

Ⓕ $\frac{1}{4} < \frac{5}{8}$

Ⓖ $\frac{1}{4} > \frac{5}{8}$

5.

Ⓐ $\frac{3}{8} < \frac{2}{3}$

Ⓑ $\frac{3}{8} > \frac{2}{3}$

GO →

Number, Operation, and Quantitative Reasoning

Objective
1

Expectation: compare and order fractions using pictorial models.

6.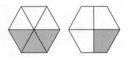

    (F) $\dfrac{4}{9} < \dfrac{2}{3}$

    (G) $\dfrac{4}{9} > \dfrac{2}{3}$

7.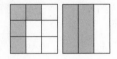

    (A) $\dfrac{3}{6} < \dfrac{1}{4}$

    (B) $\dfrac{3}{6} > \dfrac{1}{4}$

8.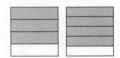

    (F) $\dfrac{3}{4} < \dfrac{4}{5}$

    (G) $\dfrac{3}{4} > \dfrac{4}{5}$

9.

    (A) $\dfrac{3}{4} < \dfrac{1}{6}$

    (B) $\dfrac{3}{4} > \dfrac{1}{6}$

10. Which figure has the same shaded area as figure A?

Figure A

(F)

(G)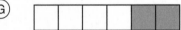

(H)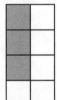

(J)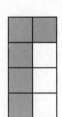

STOP

Number, Operation, and Quantitative Reasoning

Objective 1 *Expectation:* relate decimals to fractions that name tenths and hundredths using models.

DIRECTIONS: Draw a line from the number on the left to the equal number on the right.

1. 0.9

2. six tenths

3. 0.4

4. $\dfrac{32}{100}$

5. 0.7

A. seven tenths

B. $\dfrac{9}{10}$

C. 0.32

D. 0.6

E. four tenths

6. two tenths equals

(A) 0.2

(B) 0.02

(C) $\dfrac{2}{100}$

(D) $\dfrac{10}{20}$

7. 0.11 equals

(F) one eleventh

(G) $\dfrac{11}{10}$

(H) eleven hundredths

(J) eleven tenths

8. five tenths equals

(A) $\dfrac{5}{10}$

(B) 0.05

(C) $\dfrac{5}{100}$

(D) 5.0

9. Which number is not equal to one half?

(F) $\dfrac{1}{2}$

(G) 0.5

(H) $\dfrac{1}{3}$

(J) 0.50

10. Which number is not equal to 1.25?

(A) one and one fourth

(B) $1\dfrac{1}{4}$

(C) $\dfrac{5}{4}$

(D) $\dfrac{12}{50}$

11. Which number is not equal to one and three quarters?

(F) $\dfrac{9}{4}$

(G) $\dfrac{7}{4}$

(H) $1\dfrac{3}{4}$

(J) 1.75

12. Which fraction and decimal set below shows equal amounts?

(A) $\dfrac{5}{10}$ and 0.5

(B) $\dfrac{3}{4}$ and 0.34

(C) $\dfrac{1}{2}$ and 0.25

(D) $\dfrac{2}{10}$ and 0.02

STOP

Number, Operation, and Quantitative Reasoning

Objective 1

Expectation: *use addition and subtraction to solve problems involving whole numbers*

Clue The answer in an addition problem is always larger than the numbers being added. The answer in a subtraction problem is always smaller than the larger number in the problem.

DIRECTIONS: Choose the best answer.

1. Find 6.89 + 3.00.
   - (A) 3.89
   - (B) 3.98
   - (C) 0.88
   - (D) 9.89

2. Find 925 − 6.
   - (F) 919
   - (G) 931
   - (H) 325
   - (J) 1,225

3. Find 794 − 318.
   - (A) 384
   - (B) 484
   - (C) 476
   - (D) 1,112

4. Last week, the snack bar at the pool sold 1,024 hot dogs. This week, it sold 1,155 hot dogs. What was the total number of hot dogs served for the two weeks?
   - (F) 131
   - (G) 1,179
   - (H) 2,079
   - (J) 2,179

5. Use estimation to find which problem will have the greatest answer.
   - (A) 480 − 73
   - (B) 515 − 325
   - (C) 999 − 777
   - (D) 895 − 555

6. Alessandro's fourth-grade class was having its class party. There are 120 fourth-graders, but 5 were absent that day. How many students attended the class party?
   - (F) 115
   - (G) 125
   - (H) 24
   - (J) 105

7. Seven plus what number equals 71?
   - (A) 10
   - (B) 78
   - (C) 64
   - (D) 1

8. Find 1.5 + 2.9.
   - (F) 1.4
   - (G) 4.4
   - (H) 1.19
   - (J) 3.4

GO →

Number, Operation, and Quantitative Reasoning

Objective 1

Expectation: *use addition and subtraction to solve problems involving whole numbers*

DIRECTIONS: Choose the best answer.

9. Find 46 + 21.
- (A) 4,621
- (B) 67
- (C) 76
- (D) 25

10. Find 24 + 15.
- (F) 11
- (G) 9
- (H) 39
- (J) 2415

11. Find 98 − 52.
- (A) 46
- (B) 150
- (C) 9852
- (D) 33

12. Find 33 + 26.
- (F) 55
- (G) 59
- (H) 19
- (J) 7

13. Find 846 − 123.
- (A) 846
- (B) 736
- (C) 723
- (D) 733

14. Find 388 + 639.
- (F) 911
- (G) 1,017
- (H) 1,111
- (J) 1,027

15. Find 736 − 595.
- (A) 141
- (B) 131
- (C) 132
- (D) 261

16. Find 987 + 223.
- (F) 1,020
- (G) 1,450
- (H) 1,210
- (J) 1,200

17. Find 888 − 292.
- (A) 586
- (B) 596
- (C) 1,180
- (D) 576

18. Find 123 + 1,054.
- (F) 1,731
- (G) 1,177
- (H) 697
- (J) 1,687

STOP

Number, Operation, and Quantitative Reasoning

Objective 1

Expectation: add and subtract decimals to the hundredths place using pictorial models.

DIRECTIONS: Decimal squares can be used to add and subtract decimal numbers. If a whole square is divided into 100 equal parts, then each part = 1/100 or 0.01. Use the decimal squares below to find the answers to the addition and subtraction problems.

1.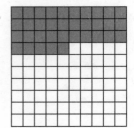

- Ⓐ 0.5
- Ⓑ 0.05
- Ⓒ 5
- Ⓓ 50

2.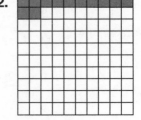

- Ⓕ 0.20
- Ⓖ 0.16
- Ⓗ 16
- Ⓙ 2.0

3.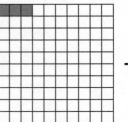

- Ⓐ 1.61
- Ⓑ 50.1
- Ⓒ 0.91
- Ⓓ 0.61

4.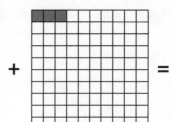

- Ⓕ 0.15
- Ⓖ 0.21
- Ⓗ 1.5
- Ⓙ 0.1

5.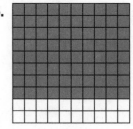

- Ⓐ 0.55
- Ⓑ 5.5
- Ⓒ 0.5
- Ⓓ 55

6.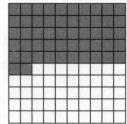

- Ⓕ 3.7
- Ⓖ 0.57
- Ⓗ 0.47
- Ⓙ 0.27

STOP

Number, Operation, and Quantitative Reasoning

Objective 1

Expectation: *model factors and products using arrays and area models*

---

1. 54 chairs need to be arranged in equal rows. Which of the following does not represent a possible arrangement?

   - (A) 9×6
   - (B) 5×4
   - (C) 3×18
   - (D) 2×27

2. 20 desks need to be arranged in equal rows. Which of the following does not represent a possible arrangement?

   - (F) 20×1
   - (G) 4×5
   - (H) 2×10
   - (J) 4×4

3. A room is 48 square feet. Which of the following does not represent possible measurements for the room?

   - (A) 3×18
   - (B) 6×8
   - (C) 2×24
   - (D) 4×12

4. 36 desks need to be arranged in equal rows. Which of the following does not represent a possible arrangement?

   - (F) 3×11
   - (G) 2×18
   - (H) 6×6
   - (J) $2 \times 2 \times 3 \times 3$

5. 16 cans need to be arranged in equal rows. Which of the following does not represent a possible arrangement?

   - (A) 1×16
   - (B) 3×8
   - (C) 4×4
   - (D) $2 \times 2 \times 2 \times 2$

6. 32 desks need to be arranged in equal rows. Which of the following does not represent a possible arrangement?

   - (F) 4×8
   - (G) 2×16
   - (H) 1×32
   - (J) $2 \times 2 \times 2 \times 2$

7. A room is 64 square feet. Which of the following does not represent possible measurements for the room?

   - (A) 2×32
   - (B) 6×16
   - (C) 8×8
   - (D) $2 \times 2 \times 2 \times 2 \times 2 \times 2$

8. A room is 81 square feet. Which of the following does not represent possible measurements for the room?

   - (F) 4×21
   - (G) 9×9
   - (H) 27×3
   - (J) $9 \times 3 \times 3$

STOP

Number, Operation, and Quantitative Reasoning

Objective 1

Expectation: *represent multiplication and division situations in picture, word and number form*

Clue   You can check your answers in a division problem by multiplying your answer by the divisor.

DIRECTIONS: Choose the best answer.

1. **Which of these is the best estimate of 767 ÷ 7 = _____ ?**
   - (A) 10
   - (B) 11
   - (C) 100
   - (D) 110

2. **Find 185 ÷ 5.**
   - (F) 37
   - (G) 36
   - (H) 180
   - (J) 190

3. **Find 88 ÷ 8.**
   - (A) 8
   - (B) 0
   - (C) 1
   - (D) 11

4. **Find 46 × 82.**
   - (F) 3,772
   - (G) 3,672
   - (H) 3,662
   - (J) 128

5. **Find 444 ÷ 6.**
   - (A) 78
   - (B) 63
   - (C) 74
   - (D) 64

6. **Find 12 × 12.**
   - (F) 240
   - (G) 144
   - (H) 140
   - (J) 24

7. **Find 304 × 57.**
   - (A) 361
   - (B) 247
   - (C) 17,328
   - (D) 19,380

8. **Find 42 ÷ 7.**
   - (F) 49
   - (G) 294
   - (H) 35
   - (J) 6

9. **Find 145 × 32.**
   - (A) 4,640
   - (B) 725
   - (C) 177
   - (D) 4,760

10. **Find 464 ÷ 4.**
    - (F) 460
    - (G) 468
    - (H) 116
    - (J) 232

STOP

114

Number, Operation, and Quantitative Reasoning

Objective
1
Expectation: *recall and apply multiplication facts through 12 x 12*

DIRECTIONS: Choose the best answer.

1. A certain factory operates two 8-hour shifts each day. How many hours does the factory operate each day?

   (A) 16
   (B) 8
   (C) 2
   (D) 10

2. It takes the cleanup crew 4 hours to clean the factory after each day's work. How many hours will the cleanup crew work during a 5-day week?

   (F) 4
   (G) 5
   (H) 9
   (J) 20

3. Lauren's mother works 5 hours each day. She works 5 days each week. How many hours does she work each week?

   (A) 5
   (B) 10
   (C) 15
   (D) 25

4. It costs a company $8 an hour to operate a certain machine. How much will it cost to operate the machine for 6 hours?

   (F) $48.00
   (G) $6.00
   (H) $8.00
   (J) $14.00

5. There are 1 dozen cans of peaches in each carton. How many cans are in 2 cartons?

   (A) 2
   (B) 24
   (C) 12
   (D) 26

6. 12 cans of pineapple are in each carton. How many cans are in 3 cartons?

   (F) 12
   (G) 15
   (H) 36
   (J) 24

7. There are 1 dozen cans of pears in each carton. How many cans are in 4 cartons?

   (A) 48
   (B) 4
   (C) 12
   (D) 5

8. Ten cans of orange sections come in each carton. How many cans are in 4 cartons?

   (F) 10
   (G) 14
   (H) 40
   (J) 48

STOP

Number, Operation, and Quantitative Reasoning

Objective 1

Expectation: use multiplication to solve problems involving two-digit numbers

---

DIRECTIONS: Choose the best answer.

1. Find 78 × 84.
   - (A) 162
   - (B) 6
   - (C) 6,552
   - (D) 312

2. The area of a rectangular space is found by multiplying the length times the width. If a room is 12 feet by 15 feet, what is the area of the room?
   - (F) 180 square feet
   - (G) 60 square feet
   - (H) 1,800 square feet
   - (J) 300 square feet

3. A store manager ordered 4 cases of juice boxes. There are 6 boxes in each package and 12 packages in a case. How many juice boxes did he order all together?
   - (A) 24 boxes
   - (B) 288 boxes
   - (C) 48 boxes
   - (D) 72 boxes

4. A truck driver makes 23 trips each week. Each trip is 76 miles long. How many miles does the truck driver travel in a week?
   - (F) 1,824 miles
   - (G) 1,748 miles
   - (H) 1,520 miles
   - (J) 53 miles

5. A gas station sells an average of 847 gallons of gasoline per day. How many gallons will be sold in a typical January?
   - (A) 10,164
   - (B) 23,716
   - (C) 25,410
   - (D) 26,257

6. A sailboat takes 24 passengers on a cruise on a lake. If the sailboat makes 53 tours a month, how many people ride on the boat each month?
   - (F) 840 people
   - (G) 1,112 people
   - (H) 1,272 people
   - (J) 2,226 people

7. Lizzie is trying to figure out the area of her desk. The length is 25 inches and the width is 48 inches. What is the area of Lizzie's desk?
   - (A) 1,200 square inches
   - (B) 1,125 square inches
   - (C) 73 square inches
   - (D) 146 square inches

8. What equation would you use to find out the number of minutes in one week?
   - (F) 24 × 60
   - (G) (7 × 24) × 60
   - (H) (7 × 24) × 365
   - (J) 365 × 60

STOP

Number, Operation, and Quantitative Reasoning

Objective 1

Expectation: *use division to solve problems involving one-digit divisors*

DIRECTIONS: Choose the best answer.

1. Ms. Fava divided her class of 24 students into groups of 2 students so that each student would have a buddy. How many groups of 2 students were there?
   - (A) 2
   - (B) 48
   - (C) 12
   - (D) 22

2. Which of the following will have a remainder when divided by 6?
   - (F) 12
   - (G) 42
   - (H) 36
   - (J) 46

3. The school basketball team has scored a total of 369 points during 9 games so far this season. What was the average number of points scored per game?
   - (A) 47
   - (B) 360
   - (C) 40
   - (D) 41

4. Terrance collected 182 seashells in 7 visits to the beach. How many seashells did he collect during each visit?
   - (F) 29
   - (G) 26
   - (H) 32
   - (J) 23

5. A machine can make 1,504 parts in 8 hours. How many parts per hour can the machine make?
   - (A) 188
   - (B) 1,496
   - (C) 1,512
   - (D) 24

6. A group of 32 students went to a basketball game. They went in 4 vans that held the same number of students. How many students were in each van?
   - (F) 36
   - (G) 28
   - (H) 16
   - (J) 8

7. The computers will be available for the same number of hours each day for five days. If the computers are available for a total of 30 hours, how many hours are they available each day?
   - (A) 35
   - (B) 25
   - (C) 11
   - (D) 6

8. When Iris visited the park, she counted 96 birds in a 4-hour period. What was the average number of birds she counted in an hour?
   - (F) 24
   - (G) 29
   - (H) 92
   - (J) 100

STOP

Number, Operation, and Quantitative Reasoning

Objective 1

Expectation: round whole numbers to the nearest ten, hundred, or thousand to approximate reasonable results in problem situations

---

DIRECTIONS: Choose the best answer.

1. What is 458 rounded to the nearest ten?
   - (A) 460
   - (B) 450
   - (C) 410
   - (D) 510

2. A number rounded to the nearest ten is 550. When it is rounded to the nearest hundred, the number becomes 600. Which of these could it be?
   - (F) 554
   - (G) 545
   - (H) 559
   - (J) 549

3. What is 1,783 rounded to the nearest hundred?
   - (A) 1,700
   - (B) 1,780
   - (C) 1,800
   - (D) 1,790

4. What is 788 rounded to the nearest hundred?
   - (F) 700
   - (G) 780
   - (H) 790
   - (J) 800

5. A number rounded to the nearest ten is 350. When it is rounded to the nearest hundred, the number becomes 400. What is the number?
   - (A) 349
   - (B) 359
   - (C) 353
   - (D) 345

6. What is 365 rounded to the nearest ten?
   - (F) 400
   - (G) 360
   - (H) 370
   - (J) 300

7. What is 2,438 rounded to the nearest thousand?
   - (A) 2,000
   - (B) 3,000
   - (C) 1,000
   - (D) 2,400

8. What is 4,900,110 rounded to the nearest million?
   - (F) 4,900,000
   - (G) 4,000,000
   - (H) 5,000,000
   - (J) 4,900,100

STOP

118

Number, Operation, and Quantitative Reasoning

Objective
1
Expectation: estimate a product or quotient beyond basic facts

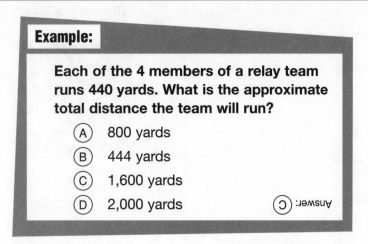

Example:

Each of the 4 members of a relay team runs 440 yards. What is the approximate total distance the team will run?

- Ⓐ 800 yards
- Ⓑ 444 yards
- Ⓒ 1,600 yards
- Ⓓ 2,000 yards

Answer: Ⓒ

DIRECTIONS: Choose the best answer.

1. Benjamin delivers 165 papers each day. Approximately how many papers does he deliver in a week?
   - Ⓐ 1,400
   - Ⓑ 700
   - Ⓒ 900
   - Ⓓ 1,500

2. A plane travels 922 kilometers in 2 hours. The same distance was traveled each hour. Approximately how far did the plane travel each hour?
   - Ⓕ 922 kilometers
   - Ⓖ 400 kilometers
   - Ⓗ 450 kilometers
   - Ⓙ 500 kilometers

3. There are 158 nails in a 1-pound pack. Approximately how many nails will be in a 5-pound pack?
   - Ⓐ 1,000
   - Ⓑ 500
   - Ⓒ 2,000
   - Ⓓ 50

4. It takes 1,212 photographs to fill 6 photo albums. Approximately how many photos are in each album?
   - Ⓕ 60
   - Ⓖ 100
   - Ⓗ 50
   - Ⓙ 200

5. A contractor estimated that it would take 2,072 bricks to build each of the 4 walls of a new house. Approximately how many bricks would it take to build all 4 walls?
   - Ⓐ 2,072
   - Ⓑ 2,000
   - Ⓒ 9,000
   - Ⓓ 8,000

6. There are 7 boxes on a truck. Each box weighs about 680 kilograms. Approximately what is the weight of all the boxes?
   - Ⓕ 4,900 kilograms
   - Ⓖ 490 kilograms
   - Ⓗ 4,200 kilograms
   - Ⓙ 4,000 kilograms

STOP

Objective

1

Mini-Test

DIRECTIONS: Choose the best answer.

1. Which of the following is equivalent to $\frac{1}{3}$?

   (A)

   (B) ✧★★★

   (C) ✧★★★★

   (D) ✧★✧★✧★

2. Which of the following can be represented by this figure?

   (F) $1\frac{1}{2}$

   (G) $1\frac{2}{3}$

   (H) $1\frac{1}{3}$

   (J) $\frac{2}{3}$

3. What is seventy-one hundredths as a fraction and as a decimal?

   (A) $7\frac{1}{100}$ 7.1

   (B) $7\frac{1}{100}$ 0.71

   (C) $\frac{71}{100}$ 7.1

   (D) $\frac{71}{100}$ 0.71

4. A room is 72 square feet. Which of the following does not represent possible measurements for the room?

   (F) 8×3

   (G) 4×18

   (H) 9×8

   (J) $2 \times 2 \times 2 \times 3 \times 3$

5. Which two shapes have an equal portion of the blocks shaded?

   1   2

   3   4

   (A) 1 and 4

   (B) 2 and 3

   (C) 2 and 4

   (D) 3 and 4

6. To be allowed into the deep end of the neighborhood pool, children must swim 12 laps across the shallow end without stopping. If Jessica has completed 8 laps, how many more laps must she swim to pass the test?

   (F) 3

   (G) 4

   (H) 8

   (J) 12

7. Forty-eight cars are parked in a parking lot. The cars are parked in 6 rows with the same number in each row. How many cars are parked in each row?

   (A) 288

   (B) 54

   (C) 8

   (D) 42

STOP

TAKS Mathematics—Objective 2

Understanding patterns, relationships, and algebraic thinking is an integral component of the foundation of algebra. Discovering patterns with whole numbers, recognizing numerical relationships, making predictions, and solving problems help build the groundwork for learning more-complex algebraic concepts. By using these patterns, students are able to recognize that combinations of numbers are interrelated. Fourth-grade students need to understand the relationship between the patterns generated by multiplication and division facts in order to solve problems. Students should be able to look at various sources of information that represent real-life situations and identify a missing piece of data. These skills are critical to the development of students' abilities to draw inferences from tables and other sources of information. With an understanding of the basic concepts included in Objective 2, students should be prepared to continue learning more-advanced algebraic ideas. In addition, the knowledge and skills in Objective 2 at fourth grade are closely aligned with the knowledge and skills in Objective 2 at fifth grade. Objective 2 combines the basic algebra concepts within the TEKS—patterns, relationships, and algebraic thinking.

The student will demonstrate an understanding of patterns, relationships, and algebraic reasoning.

(4.6) Patterns, relationships, and algebraic thinking
The student uses patterns in multiplication and division. The student is expected to
(B) solve division problems related to multiplication facts (fact families) such as $9 \times 9 = 81$ and $81 \div 9 = 9$; and *(See page 122.)*
(C) use patterns to multiply by 10 and 100. *(See page 123.)*

(4.7) Patterns, relationships, and algebraic thinking
The student uses organizational structures to analyze and describe patterns and relationships. The student is expected to
(A) describe the relationship between two sets of related data such as ordered pairs in a table. *(See page 124.)*

Number, Operation, and Quantitative Reasoning

Objective 2 **Expectation:** *solve division problems related to multiplication facts (fact families) such as 9 × 9 = 81 and 81 ÷ 9 = 9*

 Clue Sometimes you won't have to compute to find the answer to a problem. For this type of problem, it's especially important to look for key words and numbers that will help you find the correct answer.

Directions: Choose the best answer.

1. **What should replace the ■ in the number sentence below?**

   5 ■ 7 = 35

   (A) ×
   (B) ÷
   (C) +
   (D) −

2. **■ × 4 = 12**

   (F) 48
   (G) 4
   (H) 3
   (J) Not Here

3. **■ × 5 = 45**

   (A) 11
   (B) 225
   (C) 8
   (D) Not Here

4. **■ × 10 = 300**

   (F) 20
   (G) 290
   (H) 200
   (J) 30

5. **■ × 6 = 54**

   (A) 48
   (B) 60
   (C) 7
   (D) Not Here

6. **6 × ■ = 1,212**

   (F) 22
   (G) 1,218
   (H) 202
   (J) Not Here

7. **40 × ■ = 1,640**

   (A) 400
   (B) 410
   (C) 44
   (D) 41

8. **■ × 5 = 85**

   (F) 16
   (G) 17
   (H) 18
   (J) 19

STOP

Number, Operation, and Quantitative Reasoning

Objective 2

Expectation: use patterns to multiply by 10 and 100

DIRECTIONS: Replace the ■ in each number sentence below. Then find the letter in the grid that matches each answer. Write the letter that goes with each answer and solve the riddles.

Answer	0	1	2	3	4	5	6	7	8	9
Letter	A	C	E	H	I	L	M	N	O	R

1. $300 \times ■ = 2{,}700$ _____

2. $600 \times ■ = 4{,}800$ _____

3. $■00 \times 4 = 2{,}400$ _____

4. $■00 \times 9 = 1{,}800$ _____

5. $700 \times ■ = 4{,}200$ _____

6. $800 \times 5 = 4{,}■00$ _____

7. $■{,}000 \times 2 = 8{,}000$ _____

8. $■{,}000 \times 7 = 49{,}000$ _____

9. $4 \times 8{,}000 = 3■{,}000$ _____

What city likes to wander? _____ _____ _____ _____
                              1   2   3   4

What state reminds you of part of a lion? _____ _____ _____ _____ _____
                                            5   6   7   8   9

STOP

Number, Operation, and Quantitative Reasoning

Objective 2

Expectation: describe the relationship between two sets of related data such as ordered pairs in a table

DIRECTIONS: Choose the best answer to replace the box in each table.

1.

27	22
26	21
24	■

Ⓐ 22
Ⓑ 21
Ⓒ 20
Ⓓ 19

2.

2	4
5	10
7	■

Ⓕ 14
Ⓖ 16
Ⓗ 12
Ⓙ 18

3.

3	■
5	9
7	11

Ⓐ 5
Ⓑ 6
Ⓒ 7
Ⓓ 8

4.

14	7
18	■
24	12

Ⓕ 8
Ⓖ 6
Ⓗ 11
Ⓙ 9

5.

35	32
31	28
25	■

Ⓐ 30
Ⓑ 22
Ⓒ 25
Ⓓ 26

6.

47	48
26	27
13	■

Ⓕ 6
Ⓖ 26
Ⓗ 18
Ⓙ 14

7.

1	■
2	8
3	12

Ⓐ 4
Ⓑ 5
Ⓒ 6
Ⓓ 7

STOP

Objective
2

For pages 122–124

Mini-Test

DIRECTIONS: Choose the best answer.

1. $\blacksquare \times 9 = 135$
   - (A) 13
   - (B) 14
   - (C) 15
   - (D) 16

2. $\blacksquare \times 2 = 468$
   - (F) 123
   - (G) 234
   - (H) 345
   - (J) 456

3. $4 \times \blacksquare = 472$
   - (A) 118
   - (B) 116
   - (C) 120
   - (D) 122

4. $\blacksquare 00 \times 3 = 900$
   - (F) 1
   - (G) 2
   - (H) 3
   - (J) 4

5. $\blacksquare,000 \times 5 = 25,000$
   - (A) 2
   - (B) 3
   - (C) 4
   - (D) 5

6. $8,000 \times \blacksquare = 16,000$
   - (F) 2
   - (G) 3
   - (H) 1
   - (J) 4

7. $500 \times \blacksquare = 5,000$
   - (A) 20
   - (B) 10
   - (C) 30
   - (D) 2

8.

56	52
48	$\blacksquare$
35	31

   - (F) 44
   - (G) 48
   - (H) 46
   - (J) 42

9.

5	15
6	18
7	$\blacksquare$

   - (A) 14
   - (B) 21
   - (C) 28
   - (D) 35

10.

10	$\blacksquare$
8	4
6	3

   - (F) 10
   - (G) 8
   - (H) 6
   - (J) 5

STOP

TAKS Mathematics—Objective 3

The student will demonstrate an understanding of geometry and spatial reasoning.

(4.8) Geometry and spatial reasoning
The student identifies and describes lines, shapes, and solids using formal geometric language. The student is expected to

(A) identify right, acute, and obtuse angles; *(See page 127.)*

What it means:
- A right angle measures 90 degrees.
- An acute angle is less than 90 degrees.
- An obtuse angle is greater than 90 degrees.

(B) identify models of parallel and perpendicular lines; and *(See page 128.)*

What it means:
- Two lines in a plane are parallel if they never cross.
- Two lines or planes are perpendicular to each other if the angle between them is 90 degrees, or a right angle.

(C) describe shapes and solids in terms of vertices, edges, and faces *(See page 129.)*

What it means:
- A vertex of a figure is a corner. The plural of vertex is vertices. For example, a triangle has three vertices.

(4.9) Geometry and spatial reasoning
The student connects transformations to congruence and symmetry. The student is expected to

(B) use translations, reflections, and rotations to verify that two shapes are congruent; and *(See page 130.)*

(C) use reflections to verify that a shape has symmetry. *(See page 131.)*

What it means:
- A translation is a move from one place to another.
- A reflection is the production of an image by or as if by a mirror.
- A rotation is the action or process of rotating on or as if on an axis or center.
- Two figures are congruent if they are the same size and shape. They can be mirror images of each other, or turned in any direction relative to each other.
- Symmetry occurs when two halves of a figure mirror each other across a line. The line of symmetry is the line that divides the figure into two mirror images. A simple test to determine if a figure has line symmetry is to fold the figure along the supposed line of symmetry and see if the two halves of the figure coincide.

(4.10) Geometry and spatial reasoning
The student recognizes the connection between numbers and points on a number line. The student is expected to

(A) locate and name points on a number line using whole numbers, fractions such as halves and fourths, and decimals such as tenths. *(See page 132.)*

Name _____ Date _____

Geometry and Spatial Reasoning

Objective 3 *Expectation:* identify right, acute, and obtuse angles

DIRECTIONS: Choose the best answer.

1. **What type of angle is shown?**

   (A) acute
   (B) right
   (C) obtuse
   (D) none of the above

2. **What type of angle is shown?**

   (F) acute
   (G) right
   (H) obtuse
   (J) none of the above

3. **What type of angle is shown?**

   (A) acute
   (B) right
   (C) obtuse
   (D) none of the above

4. **What type of angle is shown?**

   (F) acute
   (G) right
   (H) obtuse
   (J) none of the above

5. **A 180° angle shows how much of a turn?**

   (A) $\frac{1}{4}$ turn
   (B) $\frac{1}{2}$ turn
   (C) $\frac{3}{4}$ turn
   (D) full turn

6. **A 90° angle shows how much of a turn?**

   (F) $\frac{1}{4}$ turn
   (G) $\frac{1}{2}$ turn
   (H) $\frac{3}{4}$ turn
   (J) full turn

7. **A 360° angle shows how much of a turn?**

   (A) $\frac{1}{4}$ turn
   (B) $\frac{1}{2}$ turn
   (C) $\frac{3}{4}$ turn
   (D) full turn

8. **A 270° angle shows how much of a turn?**

   (F) $\frac{1}{4}$ turn
   (G) $\frac{1}{2}$ turn
   (H) $\frac{3}{4}$ turn
   (J) full turn

STOP

Geometry and Spatial Reasoning

**Objective
3**

Expectation: *identify models of parallel and perpendicular lines*

DIRECTIONS: Choose the best answer.

1. **These lines are _____.**
   - (A) parallel
   - (B) perpendicular
   - (C) right
   - (D) none of the above

   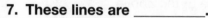

2. **These lines are _____.**
   - (F) obtuse
   - (G) perpendicular
   - (H) parallel
   - (J) none of the above

   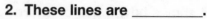

3. **These lines are _____.**
   - (A) parallel
   - (B) perpendicular
   - (C) obtuse
   - (D) none of the above

   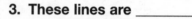

4. **These lines are _____.**
   - (F) right
   - (G) perpendicular
   - (H) parallel
   - (J) none of the above

5. **These lines are _____.**
   - (A) parallel
   - (B) perpendicular
   - (C) right
   - (D) none of the above

   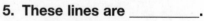

6. **These lines are _____.**
   - (F) obtuse
   - (G) perpendicular
   - (H) parallel
   - (J) none of the above

   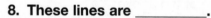

7. **These lines are _____.**
   - (A) parallel
   - (B) perpendicular
   - (C) obtuse
   - (D) none of the above

8. **These lines are _____.**
   - (F) right
   - (G) perpendicular
   - (H) parallel
   - (J) none of the above

9. **These lines are _____.**
   - (A) parallel
   - (B) perpendicular
   - (C) obtuse
   - (D) none of the above

STOP

Geometry and Spatial Reasoning

Objective 3   **Expectation:** *describe shapes and solids in terms of vertices, edges, and faces*

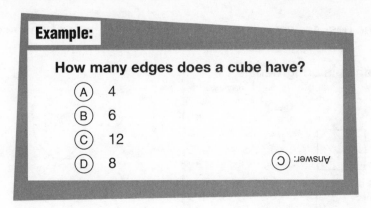

Example:

How many edges does a cube have?

- (A) 4
- (B) 6
- (C) 12
- (D) 8

Answer: (C)

DIRECTIONS: Choose the best answer.

1. Which of the figures below is a sphere?

(A)   (B)

(C)   (D)

2. How many vertices does this triangular pyramid have?

- (F) 4
- (G) 5
- (H) 6
- (J) 8

3. Which of the following is not shaped like a sphere?

- (A) basketball
- (B) beach ball
- (C) hockey puck
- (D) golf ball

4. How many faces does a cube have?

- (F) 5
- (G) 6
- (H) 7
- (J) 8

5. Which of the figures below is a cube?

(A)   (B)

(C)   (D)

6. Which of these shows the top view of the figure below?

(F)   (G)   (H)   (J)

STOP

Geometry and Spatial Reasoning

Objective 3

Expectation: use translations, reflections, and rotations to verify that two shapes are congruent

DIRECTIONS: Choose the best answer.

1. **Which pair of shapes is congruent?**

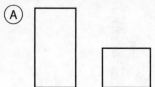

Ⓐ

Ⓑ

Ⓒ

Ⓓ

2. **Which line segment seems to be congruent to $\overline{XY}$?**

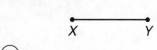

Ⓕ

Ⓖ

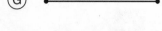

Ⓗ

Ⓙ

3. **Which pair of shapes is congruent?**

Ⓐ

Ⓑ

Ⓒ

Ⓓ

4. **Which line segment seems to be congruent to $\overline{AB}$?**

A ———— B

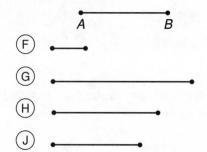

Ⓕ

Ⓖ

Ⓗ

Ⓙ

5. **Which pair of shapes is congruent?**

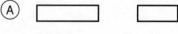

Ⓐ

Ⓑ

Ⓒ

Ⓓ

STOP

Geometry and Spatial Reasoning

Objective 3

Expectation: use reflections to verify that a shape has symmetry

 Clue   Remember that if you fold the paper on the line of symmetry, the two halves match up perfectly.

DIRECTIONS: Choose the best answer.

1. **Which of the figures below does not show a line of symmetry?**

   Ⓐ

   Ⓑ

   Ⓒ

   Ⓓ

2. **Which of these letters has a line of symmetry?**

   Ⓕ **Q**

   Ⓖ **P**

   Ⓗ **N**

   Ⓙ **M**

3. **Look at the letters below. Which one does *not* have a line of symmetry?**

   Ⓐ **O**

   Ⓑ **T**

   Ⓒ **G**

   Ⓓ **X**

4. **Which of these words contains a letter that does *not* have a line of symmetry?**

   Ⓕ **ABOUT**

   Ⓖ **BALD**

   Ⓗ **CAVE**

   Ⓙ **MOTH**

5. **Which of the figures below does not have a line of symmetry?**

   Ⓐ

   Ⓑ

   Ⓒ

   Ⓓ

STOP

Geometry and Spatial Reasoning

Objective 3

Expectation: *locate and name points on a number line using whole numbers, fractions such as halves and fourths, and decimals such as tenths*

DIRECTIONS: Use the number line for all the questions.

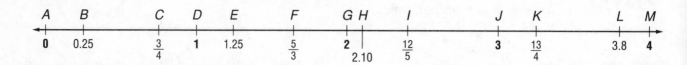

1. 3.5 would fall between which two letters?
   - (A) B and C
   - (B) E and F
   - (C) H and I
   - (D) K and L

2. How does 1.75 compare to $\frac{17}{5}$?
   - (F) less than
   - (G) same as
   - (H) greater than
   - (J) cannot compare because one is a decimal and one is a fraction

3. Which letter represents 3.25?
   - (A) C
   - (B) E
   - (C) I
   - (D) K

4. Which letter represents $\frac{21}{10}$?
   - (F) F
   - (G) G
   - (H) H
   - (J) I

5. 1.43 would fall between which two letters?
   - (A) B and C
   - (B) E and F
   - (C) H and I
   - (D) K and L

6. $\frac{1}{3}$ would fall between which two letters?
   - (F) B and C
   - (G) E and F
   - (H) H and I
   - (J) K and L

7. $2\frac{7}{8}$ would fall between which two letters?
   - (A) G and H
   - (B) H and I
   - (C) I and J
   - (D) none of these

8. Which letter represents $1\frac{2}{3}$?
   - (F) D
   - (G) E
   - (H) F
   - (J) G

STOP

Mini-Test

DIRECTIONS: Choose the best answer.

1. What type of angle is shown?

- (A) right
- (B) acute
- (C) obtuse
- (D) NG

2. These lines are _____ .

- (F) parallel
- (G) perpendicular
- (H) Not Here

3. These lines are _____ .

- (A) parallel
- (B) perpendicular
- (C) Not Here

4. How many vertices does a triangular prism have?

- (F) 9
- (G) 3
- (H) 6
- (J) 12

5. Which of the following is not shaped like a cylinder?

- (A) can of soup
- (B) tennis ball container
- (C) flag pole
- (D) window frame

6. Which of these letters has a line of symmetry?

- (F) F
- (G) G
- (H) H
- (J) J

7. Which line segment seems to be congruent to MN?

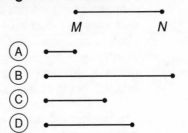

- (A)
- (B)
- (C)
- (D)

DIRECTIONS: Use the number line for exercises 8 and 9.

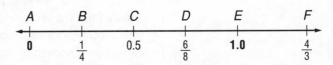

8. Which letter represents 0.75?

- (F) A
- (G) B
- (H) C
- (J) D

9. Which number is represented by the letter F?

- (A) $\frac{1}{3}$
- (B) $1\frac{1}{2}$
- (C) $1\frac{1}{3}$
- (D) $\frac{2}{3}$

STOP

TAKS Mathematics—Objective 4

Understanding the concepts and uses of measurement provides a basis for developing geometry skills. Students need to know how to reasonably estimate and accurately measure weight and capacity by using both metric and customary units. Students need to use measurement concepts to solve real life problems, including those involving length, perimeter, area, time, and temperature. With the basic concepts included in Objective 4, students will be prepared to apply measurement skills in various situations. In addition, the knowledge and skills in Objective 4 at fourth grade are closely aligned with the knowledge and skills in Objective 4 at fifth grade. Objective 4 includes the concepts within the TEKS from which an understanding of measurement is developed.

The student will demonstrate an understanding of the concepts and uses of measurement.

(4.11) Measurement
The student selects and uses appropriate units and procedures to measure weight and capacity. The student is expected to
- **(A)** estimate [and measure] weight using standard units including ounces, pounds, grams, and kilograms; and *(See page 135.)*
- **(B)** estimate [and measure] capacity using standard units including milliliters, liters, cups, pints, quarts, and gallons. *(See page 136.)*

(4.12) Measurement
The student applies measurement concepts. The student is expected to
- **(A)** measure to solve problems involving length, including perimeter, time, temperature, and area. *(See page 137.)*

Measurement

Objective 4

Expectation: estimate weight using standard units including ounces, pounds, grams, and kilograms

Example:

There are 30 tons of ore on a freight car. How many pounds of ore are on the freight car?

(A) 6,000 pounds

(B) 600 pounds

(C) 60,000 pounds

(D) 60 pounds

Answer: (C)

1. Mr. Werner bought a 5-pound roast beef. How many ounces did the roast beef weigh?

(A) 8 ounces

(B) 80 ounces

(C) 10 ounces

(D) 50 ounces

2. The load limit on a small bridge is 8 tons. What is the load limit in pounds?

(F) 16,000 pounds

(G) 1,600 pounds

(H) 160 pounds

(J) 8,000 pounds

3. A dime weighs about 2 grams. Find the weight in grams of a roll of 50 dimes.

(A) 100 grams

(B) 150 grams

(C) 200 grams

(D) 20 grams

4. Jackie's baby weighed 112 ounces when it was born. How many pounds did the baby weigh?

(F) 6 pounds

(G) 7 pounds

(H) 8 pounds

(J) 9 pounds

5. A truck was loaded with 6,000 pounds of cargo. How many tons were on the truck?

(A) 1 ton

(B) 2 tons

(C) 3 tons

(D) 4 tons

6. The dog weighed 15 pounds. How many ounces did the dog weigh?

(F) 240 ounces

(G) 150 ounces

(H) 300 ounces

(J) 280 ounces

STOP

Measurement

Objective 4

Expectation: *estimate capacity using standard units including milliliters, liters, cups, pints, quarts, and gallons*

DIRECTIONS: Choose the best answer.

1. **A restaurant served 128 pints of milk in one day. How many quarts of milk was that?**

   - (A) 64 quarts
   - (B) 32 quarts
   - (C) 96 quarts
   - (D) 16 quarts

2. **How many gallons of milk did the restaurant in question 1 serve?**

   - (F) 64 gallons
   - (G) 32 gallons
   - (H) 96 gallons
   - (J) 16 gallons

1 L   800 mL

3. **How many milliliters does the carton above hold?**

   - (A) 100 milliliters
   - (B) 10 milliliters
   - (C) 1,000 milliliters
   - (D) 10,000 milliliters

4. **Which container holds more liquid?**

   - (F) The carton holds more liquid.
   - (G) The bottle holds more liquid.

5. **A small milk carton holds 236 milliliters of milk. Approximately how many liters of milk are in 8 cartons?**

   - (A) 1 liters
   - (B) 2 liters
   - (C) 3 liters
   - (D) 4 liters

6. **There are 6 pints of lemonade in a picnic cooler. How many 1-cup containers can be filled using the lemonade in the cooler?**

   - (F) 3 cups
   - (G) 6 cups
   - (H) 12 cups
   - (J) 15 cups

7. **The cooling system on a car holds 16 quarts. How many gallons does it hold?**

   - (A) 94 gallons
   - (B) 32 gallons
   - (C) 8 gallons
   - (D) 4 gallons

8. **How many pints does the cooling system in question 7 hold?**

   - (F) 94 pints
   - (G) 32 pints
   - (H) 8 pints
   - (J) 4 pints

STOP

Name _____ Date _____

Measurement

Objective 4

Expectation: measure to solve problems involving length, including perimeter, time, temperature, and area

---

DIRECTIONS: Choose the best answer.

1. A rectangle has a length of 2 and a width of 27. What is the perimeter?
   - (A) 29
   - (B) 58
   - (C) 25
   - (D) 54

2. A rectangle has a length of 3 and a width of 24. What is the perimeter?
   - (F) 54
   - (G) 27
   - (H) 21
   - (J) 75

3. A rectangle has a length of 16 and a width of 2. What is the area?
   - (A) 18
   - (B) 14
   - (C) 32
   - (D) 8

4. A rectangle has a length of 9 and a width of 9. What is the area?
   - (F) 18
   - (G) 81
   - (H) 45
   - (J) 27

5. A rectangle has a length of 10 and a width of 8. What is the area?
   - (A) 18
   - (B) 80
   - (C) 2
   - (D) 4

6. A rectangle has a length of 8 and a width of 9. What is the perimeter?
   - (F) 17
   - (G) 1
   - (H) 80
   - (J) 34

7. Look at the thermometers. How did the temperature change between Saturday and Sunday? On Sunday it was _____ .

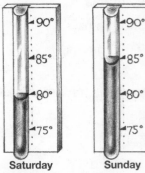

   - (A) 5 degrees cooler than on Saturday
   - (B) 10 degrees cooler than on Saturday
   - (C) 5 degrees warmer than on Saturday
   - (D) 10 degrees warmer than on Saturday

8. Toby left his house for school at 7:35 A.M. He arrived to school at 7:50 A.M. How many minutes did it take Toby to get to school?
   - (F) 15 minutes
   - (G) 20 minutes
   - (H) 25 minutes
   - (J) 10 minutes

Name _____ Date _____

Mini-Test

DIRECTIONS: Choose the best answer.

1. A truck has 6 tons of cargo. How many pounds is that?

   Ⓐ 12,000 pounds

   Ⓑ 1,200 pounds

   Ⓒ 120 pounds

   Ⓓ 12 pounds

2. 9 kilograms is how many grams?

   Ⓕ 90,000 grams

   Ⓖ 90 grams

   Ⓗ 900 grams

   Ⓙ 9,000 grams

3. 45,000 grams is how many kilograms?

   Ⓐ 45 kg

   Ⓑ 450 kg

   Ⓒ 4,500 kg

   Ⓓ 4.5 kg

4. Barb used 8 liters of water when she washed her hands and face. How many milliliters of water did she use?

   Ⓕ 8 milliliters

   Ⓖ 80 milliliters

   Ⓗ 800 milliliters

   Ⓙ 8,000 milliliters

5. There are 28 students in Barb's class. Suppose each student uses 8 liters of water. How many liters would be used?

   Ⓐ 64 liters

   Ⓑ 224 liters

   Ⓒ 16 liters

   Ⓓ 23 liters

6. How many quarts of water would be needed to fill a 10-gallon aquarium?

   Ⓕ 4 quarts

   Ⓖ 40 quarts

   Ⓗ 20 quarts

   Ⓙ 60 quarts

7. The lunchroom served 168 pints of milk at lunch. How many quarts of milk was this?

   Ⓐ 16 quarts

   Ⓑ 21 quarts

   Ⓒ 42 quarts

   Ⓓ 84 quarts

8. The area of a rectangle is 943 square inches. The length of the rectangle is 41 inches. What is the width of the rectangle?

   Ⓕ 24 inches

   Ⓖ 32 inches

   Ⓗ 23 inches

   Ⓙ 18 inches

9. What is the perimeter of a triangular room if all the sides are 4.5 meters long?

   Ⓐ 9 meters

   Ⓑ 18 meters

   Ⓒ 13.5 meters

   Ⓓ 22.5 meters

10. Rachelle started her homework at 3:00. She finished at 5:15. For how long did she work?

    Ⓕ 3 hours

    Ⓖ 2 hours

    Ⓗ 140 minutes

    Ⓙ 2 hours, 15 minutes

TAKS Mathematics—Objective 5

Understanding probability and statistics will help students become informed consumers of data and information. In experimental situations such as coin tossing, students should determine the probability that an event will occur and transfer this knowledge to current issues. By recognizing all the possible outcomes in a specific situation, students will be able to predict the results of probability experiments. Students will learn to interpret various bar graphs and understand the significance of the displayed information so that it can be applied to real-world situations. It is important for students to correctly interpret information from graphic formats in order to communicate that information effectively. The knowledge and skills contained in Objective 5 are essential for processing everyday information. In addition, the knowledge and skills in Objective 5 at fourth grade are closely aligned with the knowledge and skills in Objective 5 at fifth grade.

Objective 5 includes the concepts within the TEKS that form the groundwork for an understanding of probability and statistics.

The student will demonstrate an understanding of probability and statistics.

(4.13) Probability and statistics

The student solves problems by collecting, organizing, displaying, and interpreting sets of data. The student is expected to

(A) list all possible outcomes of a probability experiment such as tossing a coin; *(See page 140.)*

(B) use a pair of numbers to compare favorable outcomes to all possible outcomes such as four heads out of six tosses of a coin; and *(See page 141.)*

(C) interpret bar graphs. *(See page 142.)*

© McGraw-Hill Children's Publishing

Probability and Statistics

Objective 5

Expectation: list all possible outcomes of a probability experiment such as tossing a coin

---

DIRECTIONS: Choose the best answer.

Venita is making a sandwich. She has white, wheat, and Italian bread. She can choose from ham, roast beef, and turkey for the meat. Use the following tree diagram to answer questions 1–3.

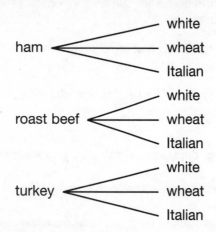

1. **How many choices does Venita have?**
   - (A) 12
   - (B) 9
   - (C) 3
   - (D) 6

2. **If Venita decides she doesn't want wheat bread, how many choices does she have?**
   - (F) 12
   - (G) 9
   - (H) 3
   - (J) 6

3. **Which of the following is not an option?**
   - (A) roast beef on rye
   - (B) turkey on Italian
   - (C) ham on wheat
   - (D) turkey on white

Scott was choosing what to wear one morning. He has jeans or khakis for pants and red, blue, and green shirts. Use the following tree diagram to answer questions 4–6.

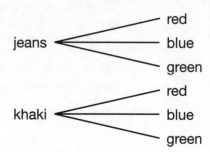

4. **How many options does Scott have for outfits?**
   - (F) 6
   - (G) 3
   - (H) 8
   - (J) 2

5. **Which of the following is not an option?**
   - (A) jeans with red shirt
   - (B) khakis with blue shirt
   - (C) jeans with yellow shirt
   - (D) khakis with green shirt

6. **If Scott decides he wants to wear his blue shirt, how many options does he have?**
   - (F) 6
   - (G) 3
   - (H) 8
   - (J) 2

Probability and Statistics

Objective 5

Expectation: use a pair of numbers to compare favorable outcomes to all possible outcomes such as four heads out of six tosses of a coin

---

DIRECTIONS: Use the following information for numbers 1–3. In a grocery bag there are 6 cans of tomato sauce, 4 cans of beans, and 9 cans of olives. All the cans are the same size.

1. If you reached into the bag without looking and picked out a can, what is the probability of picking a can of olives?

   Ⓐ $\frac{1}{2}$

   Ⓑ $\frac{1}{9}$

   Ⓒ $\frac{9}{1}$

   Ⓓ $\frac{9}{19}$

2. What is the probability of picking a can of beans?

   Ⓕ $\frac{4}{19}$

   Ⓖ $\frac{1}{4}$

   Ⓗ $\frac{4}{9}$

   Ⓙ $\frac{4}{6}$

3. What is the probability of picking a can of tomato sauce?

   Ⓐ $\frac{1}{2}$

   Ⓑ $\frac{6}{9}$

   Ⓒ $\frac{6}{19}$

   Ⓓ $\frac{4}{6}$

DIRECTIONS: Use the following information for numbers 4–6. A box contains 5 red crayons, 3 green crayons, and 2 blue crayons.

4. If you reach into the box without looking, what is the probability of picking a blue crayon?

   Ⓕ $\frac{5}{10}$

   Ⓖ $\frac{1}{5}$

   Ⓗ $\frac{2}{5}$

   Ⓙ $\frac{2}{3}$

5. What is the probability of picking a red crayon?

   Ⓐ $\frac{1}{2}$

   Ⓑ $\frac{1}{5}$

   Ⓒ $\frac{2}{5}$

   Ⓓ $\frac{2}{3}$

6. What is the probability of picking a green crayon?

   Ⓕ $\frac{3}{10}$

   Ⓖ $\frac{3}{5}$

   Ⓗ $\frac{3}{7}$

   Ⓙ $\frac{5}{3}$

STOP

Probability and Statistics

Objective 5

Expectation: *interpret bar graphs*

DIRECTIONS: Use the graph below for numbers 1–3.

Top Countries Generating Hydroelectric Power

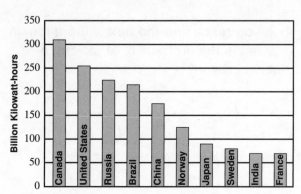

1. **Which country produces the least amount of hydroelectricity?**

   (A) Brazil

   (B) China

   (C) India

   (D) Canada

2. **Which country produces more hydroelectricity than Brazil and less than the United States?**

   (F) Russia

   (G) China

   (H) Canada

   (J) Brazil

3. **Which two countries produce about the same amount of hydroelectricity?**

   (A) India and France

   (B) Russia and Brazil

   (C) Japan and Sweden

   (D) Sweden and India

DIRECTIONS: Use the graph below for numbers 4–6.

Number of Students at Highview School

Grade Level	Number of Students
Kindergarten	♀♀♀♀♀♀♀♀
1st Grade	♀♀♀♀♀♀♀♀♀♀♀♀
2nd Grade	♀♀♀♀♀♀♀
3rd Grade	♀♀♀♀♀♀♀♀
4th Grade	♀♀♀♀♀♀♀♀♀♀♀♀
5th Grade	♀♀♀♀♀♀♀

Key: ♀ = 5 students

4. **How many students attend Highview School?**

   (F) 275

   (G) 290

   (H) 315

   (J) 192

5. **How many Highview students are fourth graders?**

   (A) 30

   (B) 40

   (C) 50

   (D) 60

6. **What is the mean or average number of students in each grade at Highview? (round to the nearest one)**

   (F) 41

   (G) 46

   (H) 38

   (J) 52

STOP

Name _____   Date _____

Objective
5

Mini-Test

DIRECTIONS: Choose the best answer.

Edison was wrapping a present. He had blue, silver, and gold ribbon and white, red, and black wrapping paper. Use the following tree diagram to answer questions 1–3.

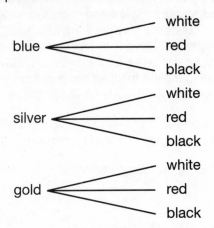

blue — white / red / black
silver — white / red / black
gold — white / red / black

1. **How many wrapping options did Edison have?**
   - (A) 12
   - (B) 3
   - (C) 9
   - (D) 6

2. **Which of the following is not an option?**
   - (F) silver ribbon on white paper
   - (G) blue ribbon on yellow paper
   - (H) blue ribbon on red paper
   - (J) gold ribbon on black paper

3. **If Edison decides not to use the black paper, how many options does he have?**
   - (A) 12
   - (B) 3
   - (C) 9
   - (D) 6

DIRECTIONS: Use the following information for questions 4–6. A bag contains 7 red marbles, 5 green marbles, 3 white marbles, and 2 gold marbles.

4. **If you reach into the bag without looking, what is the probability of picking a red marble?**
   - (F) $\frac{7}{10}$
   - (G) $\frac{7}{17}$
   - (H) $\frac{7}{8}$
   - (J) $\frac{7}{9}$

5. **What is the probability of picking a gold marble?**
   - (A) $\frac{2}{17}$
   - (B) $\frac{2}{7}$
   - (C) $\frac{2}{5}$
   - (D) $\frac{2}{3}$

6. **What is the probability of picking a green marble?**
   - (F) $\frac{5}{7}$
   - (G) $\frac{5}{5}$
   - (H) $\frac{5}{15}$
   - (J) $\frac{5}{17}$

STOP

TAKS Mathematics—Objective 6

Knowledge and understanding of underlying processes and mathematical tools are critical for students to be able to apply mathematics in their everyday lives. Problems found in everyday life often require the use of multiple concepts and skills. Students should be able to recognize mathematics as it occurs in real-life problem situations, generalize from mathematical patterns and sets of examples, select an appropriate approach to solving a problem, solve the problem, and then determine whether the answer is reasonable. Expressing these problem situations in mathematical language and symbols is essential for finding solutions to real-life questions. These concepts allow students to communicate clearly and to use logical reasoning to make sense of their world. Students can then connect the concepts they have learned in mathematics to other disciplines and to higher mathematics. Through understanding the basic ideas found in Objective 6, students will be able to analyze and solve real-world problems. In addition, the knowledge and skills in Objective 6 at fourth grade are closely aligned with the knowledge and skills in Objective 6 at fifth grade.

Objective 6 incorporates the underlying processes and mathematical tools within the TEKS that are used to find mathematical solutions to real-world problems.

The student will demonstrate an understanding of the mathematical processes and tools used in problem solving.

(4.14) Underlying processes and mathematical tools
The student applies Grade 4 mathematics to solve problems connected to everyday experiences and activities in and outside of school. The student is expected to
- **(A)** identify the mathematics in everyday situations; *(See page 145.)*
- **(B)** use a problem-solving model that incorporates understanding the problem, making a plan, carrying out the plan, and evaluating the solution for reasonableness; and *(See page 146.)*
- **(C)** select or develop an appropriate problem-solving strategy, including drawing a picture, looking for a pattern, systematic guessing and checking, acting it out, making a table, working a simpler problem, or working backwards to solve a problem. *(See page 147.)*

(4.15) Underlying processes and mathematical tools
The student communicates about Grade 4 mathematics using informal language. The student is expected to
- **(B)** relate informal language to mathematical language and symbols.
  (See page 148.)

(4.16) Underlying processes and mathematical tools
The student uses logical reasoning to make sense of his or her world. The student is expected to
- **(A)** make generalizations from patterns or sets of examples and nonexamples.
  (See page 149.)

Underlying Processes and Mathematical Tools

Objective 6

Expectation: identify the mathematics in everyday situations

DIRECTIONS: Choose the best answer.

1. There are 62 students on a class trip. They are taking a bus to the nature park. The ride to the park takes 25 minutes and the ride home takes 30 minutes. Lunch at the park costs $3.25 per child. How much does it cost to get into the park?

- (A) $201.50
- (B) $50.00
- (C) $120.25
- (D) Not enough information

2. The school play ran for 3 nights, and 345 people attended each night. Tickets cost $4.25 each. How much money did the school play make?

- (F) $1,239.50
- (G) $1,466.25
- (H) $1,035.00
- (J) $4,398.75

3. Jesse bought a pack of cards for $1.25 and a baseball for $8.39. He has $5.36 left over. With how much money did he start?

- (A) $20.00
- (B) $9.64
- (C) $1.78
- (D) $15.00

4. There are 21 fish in every square yard of water in a lake. If the lake is 812 square yards, how many fish are in the lake?

- (F) 17,052
- (G) 23,708
- (H) 29,987
- (J) 14,879

5. Mona started her chores at 3:30 P.M. She needed to take out the garbage, wash the dishes, water the houseplants, feed the dog, and clean up her room. Mona finished her chores just as her dad came home at 5:20 P.M. How long did it take Mona to do her chores?

- (A) 50 minutes
- (B) 2 hours
- (C) 1 hour, 50 minutes
- (D) None of these

6. If the temperature in the morning is 56°F, what will the temperature be when it rises 25° this afternoon?

- (F) 78°F
- (G) 76°F
- (H) 81°F
- (J) 85°F

STOP

Underlying Processes and Mathematical Tools

Objective 6

Expectation: use a problem-solving model that incorporates understanding the problem, making a plan, carrying out the plan, and evaluating the solution for reasonableness.

 Before you choose an answer, ask yourself, "Does this answer make sense?"

DIRECTIONS: Choose the best answer.

1. **Which of the following would you probably measure in feet?**

   (A) length of a pencil

   (B) distance between two cities

   (C) amount of juice left in a bottle

   (D) the length of a couch

2. **You are mailing in your brother's college application today. It is a regular letter size. You must make sure you have enough postage. How much do you think it weighs?**

   (F) 1 pound

   (G) 8 pounds

   (H) 1 ounce

   (J) 8 ounces

3. **Leslie is making punch in a very large punch bowl. Orange juice comes in different-sized containers. Which size container should she buy in order to purchase the fewest number of containers?**

   (A) a one-cup container

   (B) a one-gallon container

   (C) a one-pint container

   (D) a one-quart container

4. **Trina's family has two dogs. Pepper weighs 31 pounds. Salt weighs 28 pounds. To the nearest ten pounds, how much is the combined weight of the two dogs?**

   (F) 59

   (G) 31

   (H) 28

   (J) 60

5. **Mr. Cook was 25 years old when Mary was born. How old will he be when Mary has her thirteenth birthday?**

   (A) 38

   (B) 12

   (C) 25

   (D) 13

6. **Marcos has $47.82. He plans to spend $25 on presents. How much money will he have left, to the nearest dollar?**

   (F) $22

   (G) $22.82

   (H) $23

   (J) $25

STOP

Underlying Processes and Mathematical Tools

Objective 6

Expectation: select or develop an appropriate problem-solving strategy, including drawing a picture, looking for a pattern, systematic guessing and checking, acting it out, making a table, working a simpler problem, or working backwards to solve a problem.

DIRECTIONS: Choose the best answer.

1. **You have coins that total $1.23. What coins do you have?**

   (A) 10 dimes, 1 nickel, 3 pennies

   (B) 3 quarter, 3 dimes, 3 pennies

   (C) 4 quarters, 1 dimes, 2 nickels, 3 pennies

   (D) 4 quarters, 3 dimes, 3 pennies

2. **The sum of each column in the number pattern below equals 21. What numbers are missing?**

3	5	2	1	6
2	7	8	9	1
9	8	4	6	7
___	1	7	___	7

   (F) 6 and 8

   (G) 7 and 5

   (H) 1 and 7

   (J) 4 and 3

3. **A shape has 4 sides. Two sides are the same length and one corner is 90 degrees. What is the shape?**

   (A) parallelogram

   (B) rectangle

   (C) triangle

   (D) Not enough information

4. **Kim made one straight cut across the trapezoid as shown. Which pair of figures could be the two cut pieces of the trapezoid?**

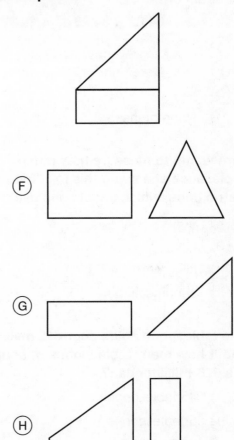

STOP

Underlying Processes and Mathematical Tools

Objective
6

Expectation: relate informal language to mathematical language and symbols

---

DIRECTIONS: Choose the best answer.

1. **Which symbol below best completes the equation?**

    84.62 ■ 84.26

    (A) >

    (B) =

    (C) <

    (D) None of these

2. **Sara wants to measure how much applesauce she made this fall. If she uses metric units, which should she use?**

    (F) gram

    (G) liter

    (H) kilogram

    (J) centimeter

3. **One tablespoon holds about 15 milliliters. About how many tablespoons of soup are in a 225-milliliter can?**

    (A) 45 tablespoons

    (B) 5 tablespoons

    (C) 3,375 tablespoons

    (D) 15 tablespoons

4. **Find the weight in kilograms of a shipment of 30 math books if each book weighs 2 kg.**

    (F) 10 kg

    (G) 90 kg

    (H) 9 kg

    (J) 60 kg

5. **The temperature on Saturday was 78 degrees. On Sunday it was 12 degrees warmer. What was the temperature on Sunday?**

    (A) 66 degrees

    (B) 56 degrees

    (C) 90 degrees

    (D) 86 degrees

6. **Which of these has the greatest volume?**

    (F) 4 quarts

    (G) 2 gallons

    (H) 8 pints

    (J) 17 cups

7. **Which of the following sets of figures shows $\frac{1}{3}$ shaded?**

    (A) ① ① ① ① ❶ ❶ ❶

    (B) ① ① ❶ ❶ ❶ ❶

    (C) ① ❶ ① ❶ ① ❶

    (D) ① ① ❶ ① ① ❶

STOP

Underlying Processes and Mathematical Tools

Objective 6

Expectation: *make generalizations from patterns or sets of examples and non-examples*

DIRECTIONS: Choose the best answer.

1. **Which of these numbers is even and a multiple of 12?**
   - (A) 34
   - (B) 145
   - (C) 144
   - (D) 148

2. **The sum of two numbers is 21 and their product is 98. What are the 2 numbers?**
   - (F) 12 and 8
   - (G) 14 and 7
   - (H) 77 and 21
   - (J) 7 and 9

3. **There are two numbers whose product is 98 and quotient is 2. What are the two numbers?**
   - (A) 49 and 8
   - (B) 14 and 2
   - (C) 14 and 7
   - (D) 96 and 2

4. **In this pyramid, each number is the product of the two numbers directly below it. Which number is missing?**

   ```
           48
        8   ___
      4    2    3
   ```
   - (F) 6
   - (G) 4
   - (H) 8
   - (J) None of these

5. **How many hundreds are in 100,000?**
   - (A) 10
   - (B) 100,000
   - (C) 100
   - (D) 1,000

6. **Nicolas has a water bottle that holds 2 gallons. Which of the following would fill it?**
   - (F) 4 cups
   - (G) 3 pints
   - (H) 8 quarts
   - (J) 1 liter

7. **Larry, Carey, and Harry went out for lunch. Each friend ordered a salad. The choices were egg, tuna, and chicken. Carey won't eat egg. Larry never orders tuna. Harry only likes chicken. Each friend ate something different. Who ordered tuna?**
   - (A) Larry
   - (B) Carey
   - (C) Harry
   - (D) Not enough information

8. **There were 488 balloons decorating the gymnasium for a party. There were 97 students at the party. If each student brought home an equal number of balloons after the party, how many balloons were left over?**
   - (F) 3 balloons
   - (G) 46 balloons
   - (H) 12 balloons
   - (J) None of these

STOP

Objective

6

Mini-Test

DIRECTIONS: Choose the best answer.

1. A farmer is selling fruits and vegetables. She has 32 peaches, 48 potatoes, 13 heads of lettuce, 11 melons, 20 onions, and 50 plums. How many fruits does the farmer have?

   (A) 93

   (B) 174

   (C) 81

   (D) 82

2. An auto dealer hopes to sell twice as many cars this year as last year. He sold 1,056 cars last year. To the nearest hundred, how many cars does the dealer hope to sell this year?

   (F) 2,100

   (G) 2,000

   (H) 1,100

   (J) 500

3. In one hour, 560 loaves of bread can be baked. How many loaves can be baked in 112 hours, to the nearest hundred?

   (A) 62,700

   (B) 63,000

   (C) 62,000

   (D) 600

4. Each side of a square is an odd number of inches. The total length of its sides will be _____ .

   (F) an even number

   (G) an odd number

   (H) always greater than 40 inches

   (J) either an even or an odd number

5. When you subtract 5 from a number larger than 10, the answer will be _____.

   (A) odd or even

   (B) always less than 10

   (C) always even

   (D) always odd

6. Six musicians gave a concert. There were 273 people in the audience. 9 people left early. 15 people were sitting in the front row. Which number sentence shows how many people were in the audience until the end?

   (F) 9 × 15

   (G) 271 + 9 + 15

   (H) 273 + 9

   (J) 273 − 9

7. Choose the operation sign that makes
   3 ■ 4 = 12
   a true statement.

   (A) +

   (B) −

   (C) ×

   (D) ÷

8. What is the value of 1 nickel, 2 dimes, 1 quarter, and 1 penny?

   (F) $0.56

   (G) $0.50

   (H) $0.51

   (J) $0.57

150

How Am I Doing?

Objective 1 Mini-Test

Page 120

Number Correct

7 answers correct	**Great Job!** Move on to the section test on page 153.
5–6 answers correct	**You're almost there!** But you still need a little practice. Review practice pages 104–119 before moving on to the section test on page 153.
0–4 answers correct	**Oops!** Time to review what you have learned and try again. Review the practice section on pages 104–119. Then retake the test on page 120. Now move on to the section test on page 153.

Objective 2 Mini-Test

Page 125

Number Correct

9–10 answers correct	**Awesome!** Move on to the section test on page 153.
6–8 answers correct	**You're almost there!** But you still need a little practice. Review practice pages 122–124 before moving on to the section test on page 153.
0–5 answers correct	**Oops!** Time to review what you have learned and try again. Review the practice section on pages 122–124. Then retake the test on page 125. Now move on to the section test on page 153.

Objective 3 Mini-Test

Page 133

Number Correct

8–9 answers correct	**Great Job!** Move on to the section test on page 153.
5–7 answers correct	**You're almost there!** But you still need a little practice. Review practice pages 127–132 before moving on to the section test on page 153.
0–4 answers correct	**Oops!** Time to review what you have learned and try again. Review the practice section on pages 127–132. Then retake the test on page 133. Now move on to the section test on page 153.

How Am I Doing?

Objective 4 Mini-Test

Page 138

Number Correct

9–10 answers correct	**Great Job!** Move on to the section test on page 153.
6–8 answers correct	**You're almost there!** But you still need a little practice. Review practice pages 135–137 before moving on to the section test on page 153.
0–5 answers correct	**Oops!** Time to review what you have learned and try again. Review the practice section on pages 135–137. Then retake the test on page 138. Now move on to the section test on page 153.

Objective 5 Mini-Test

Page 143

Number Correct

6 answers correct	**Awesome!** Move on to the section test on page 153.
4–5 answers correct	**You're almost there!** But you still need a little practice. Review practice pages 140–142 before moving on to the section test on page 153.
0–3 answers correct	**Oops!** Time to review what you have learned and try again. Review the practice section on pages 140–142. Then retake the test on page 143. Now move on to the section test on page 153.

Objective 6 Mini-Test

Page 150

Number Correct

7–8 answers correct	**Great Job!** Move on to the section test on page 153.
5–6 answers correct	**You're almost there!** But you still need a little practice. Review practice pages 145–149 before moving on to the section test on page 153.
0–4 answers correct	**Oops!** Time to review what you have learned and try again. Review the practice section on pages 145–149. Then retake the test on page 150. Now move on to the section test on page 153.

Name _____ Date _____

Final Test for
Mathematics
for pages 104–150

DIRECTIONS: Choose the best answer.

1. What fraction of the shape is shaded?

(A) $\frac{1}{2}$

(B) $\frac{3}{4}$

(C) $\frac{7}{16}$

(D) $\frac{5}{8}$

2. Which of the following represents $1\frac{1}{3}$?

(F)

(G)

(H)

(J)

3. What math fact do the pictures below show to be true?

(A) $\frac{4}{8}$ is less than $\frac{1}{2}$

(B) $\frac{4}{8}$ is equal to $\frac{1}{2}$

(C) $\frac{4}{8}$ is greater than $\frac{1}{2}$

(D) $\frac{4}{8}$ is equal to $\frac{1}{4}$

4. Which of the following is not equal to 0.5?

(F) 0.50

(G) five tenths

(H) $\frac{1}{2}$

(J) five

5. Which fraction shows how many of the shapes are shaded?

(A) $\frac{1}{6}$

(B) $\frac{3}{5}$

(C) $\frac{7}{10}$

(D) $\frac{1}{2}$

6. Which fraction tells how much of this figure is shaded?

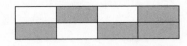

(F) $\frac{2}{3}$

(G) $\frac{3}{4}$

(H) $\frac{1}{4}$

(J) $\frac{5}{8}$

GO

7. 28 cans need to be arranged in equal rows. Which of the following does not represent a possible arrangement?

   (A) 3 × 9
   (B) 4 × 7
   (C) 2 × 14
   (D) 2 × 2 × 7

8. A trailer can carry 6 motorcycles. If there are 7 trailers, how many motorcycles can be transported?

   (F) 13
   (G) 49
   (H) 42
   (J) 67

9. If a room measures 32 feet by 45 feet, what is its area?

   (A) 1440
   (B) 77
   (C) 154
   (D) 144

10. There are 32 girls in a relay race. Four run on each team. How many teams are there?

   (F) 256
   (G) 40
   (H) 24
   (J) 8

11. What is 4,911 rounded to the nearest thousand?

   (A) 4,000
   (B) 5,000
   (C) 4,900
   (D) 4,910

12. A train can travel 97 kilometers in one hour. How far can it travel in 13 hours?

   (F) 7
   (G) 970
   (H) 291
   (J) 1,261

13. A tank contains 555 liters of oil. Nine liters of oil are used each day. Approximately how many days will the supply last?

   (A) 40
   (B) 50
   (C) 60
   (D) 70

14. ■ × 7 = 490

   (F) 70
   (G) 700
   (H) 497
   (J) NG

15.

4	7
9	12
15	■

   (A) 13
   (B) 14
   (C) 15
   (D) 18

GO

16. ■ × 500 = 2,000

    (F) 2

    (G) 3

    (H) 4

    (J) 5

17. What type of angle is shown?

    (A) right

    (B) acute

    (C) obtuse

    (D) Not Here

18. These lines are _____ .

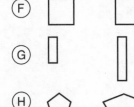

    (F) parallel

    (G) perpendicular

    (H) Not Here

19. How many edges does a trapezoid have?

    (A) 5

    (B) 4

    (C) 3

    (D) 2

20. Which pair of shapes is congruent?

21. Which of these letters does *not* have a line of symmetry?

    (A) **O**

    (B) **T**

    (C) **E**

    (D) **K**

22. What point represents $\frac{1}{2}$?

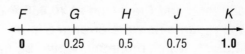

    (F) F

    (G) G

    (H) H

    (J) J

23. 16 kilograms is how many grams?

    (A) 16 grams

    (B) 160 grams

    (C) 1,600 grams

    (D) 16,000 grams

24. There are 12 cups of liquid in a container. How many 1-pint jars can be filled by using the liquid in the container?

    (F) 3 cups

    (G) 6 cups

    (H) 9 cups

    (J) 12 cups

GO

25. **A rectangle measures 8 meters by 3 meters. What is the perimeter of the rectangle?**

   (A) 22 meters

   (B) 18 meters

   (C) 11 meters

   (D) 3 meters

26. **Noriko was looking at a map of Glacier National Park. He noted the heights of five mountain peaks: Rockwell at 9,272 feet; Going-to-the-Sun at 9,642 feet; Thunderbird at 8,520 feet; Kaina at 9,489 feet; and Cleveland at 10,466 feet. If the mountains were arranged in order of height, which mountain would be in the middle?**

   (F) Kaina

   (G) Going-to-the-Sun

   (H) Thunderbird

   (J) Rockwell

27. **Which is the best way to estimate 47 × 53?**

   (A) 50 × 60

   (B) 40 × 60

   (C) 50 × 50

   (D) 40 × 50

28. **Alex's fourth-grade class was having its class party. There are 120 fourth graders, but 5 were absent that day. How many students attended the class party?**

   (F) 115

   (G) 125

   (H) 24

   (J) 105

29. **Which of the following is the closest estimate for the equation 254 ÷ 2?**

   (A) 100

   (B) 125

   (C) 500

   (D) 300

30. **Toby left his house for school at 7:35 A.M. He arrived at school at 7:50 A.M., which was 10 minutes before school started. How long before school started did Toby leave the house?**

   (F) 10 minutes

   (G) 15 minutes

   (H) 25 minutes

   (J) not enough information

31. **What is the value of 3 nickels, 4 dimes, 1 quarter, and 2 pennies?**

   (A) $0.56

   (B) $0.50

   (C) $0.82

   (D) $0.57

32. **If Jerry walked 2 miles for charity, how many feet did he walk?**

   (F) 20 feet

   (G) 6 feet

   (H) 3,520 feet

   (J) 10,560 feet

GO

33. Gerald's desk has 5 pencils, 3 erasers and 2 boxes of crayons. There are 16 crayons in each box. How many crayons does Gerald have?

(A) 30
(B) 10
(C) 26
(D) 32

34. Each day 7,500 tons of ore can be processed. How many thousands of tons of ore can be processed in 25 days?

(F) 188
(G) 187,500
(H) 188,000
(J) 8

35. Which type of graph would be best to show how the average weekly temperature changed in one town from month to month?

(A) pie chart
(B) tally chart
(C) bar graph
(D) line graph

36. A circus has 13 elephants. Twinkle weighs 8,100 pounds. Peanut weighs 11,423 pounds. Which number sentence will tell how much more Peanut weighs than Twinkle?

(F) 8,100 – 11,423
(G) 11,423 – 8,100
(H) 11,423 + 8,100
(J) 13 × 8,100

37. David scored 1,832 points on a video game. Susan scored 2 times more than David. Paul scored 234 points less than Susan. What was Paul's score?

(A) 3,320 points
(B) 3,664 points
(C) 3,430 points
(D) 468 points

38. There are 376 quarts of milk delivered to the store. How many gallons of milk was this?

(F) 94 gallons
(G) 32 gallons
(H) 8 gallons
(J) 4 gallons

39. If you burn 318 calories in 60 minutes of playing tennis, how many calories would you burn in 30 minutes?

(A) 159 calories
(B) 636 calories
(C) 258 calories
(D) 288 calories

40. Kylie ran 5 miles on Tuesday. How many feet did she run?

(F) 500 feet
(G) 10,000 feet
(H) 26,400 feet
(J) 41,250 feet

STOP

Name _____   Date _____

Final Mathematics Test
Answer Sheet

1	Ⓐ Ⓑ Ⓒ Ⓓ	21	Ⓐ Ⓑ Ⓒ Ⓓ
2	Ⓕ Ⓖ Ⓗ Ⓙ	22	Ⓕ Ⓖ Ⓗ Ⓙ
3	Ⓐ Ⓑ Ⓒ Ⓓ	23	Ⓐ Ⓑ Ⓒ Ⓓ
4	Ⓕ Ⓖ Ⓗ Ⓙ	24	Ⓕ Ⓖ Ⓗ Ⓙ
5	Ⓐ Ⓑ Ⓒ Ⓓ	25	Ⓐ Ⓑ Ⓒ Ⓓ
6	Ⓕ Ⓖ Ⓗ Ⓙ	26	Ⓕ Ⓖ Ⓗ Ⓙ
7	Ⓐ Ⓑ Ⓒ Ⓓ	27	Ⓐ Ⓑ Ⓒ Ⓓ
8	Ⓕ Ⓖ Ⓗ Ⓙ	28	Ⓕ Ⓖ Ⓗ Ⓙ
9	Ⓐ Ⓑ Ⓒ Ⓓ	29	Ⓐ Ⓑ Ⓒ Ⓓ
10	Ⓕ Ⓖ Ⓗ Ⓙ	30	Ⓕ Ⓖ Ⓗ Ⓙ
11	Ⓐ Ⓑ Ⓒ Ⓓ	31	Ⓐ Ⓑ Ⓒ Ⓓ
12	Ⓕ Ⓖ Ⓗ Ⓙ	32	Ⓕ Ⓖ Ⓗ Ⓙ
13	Ⓐ Ⓑ Ⓒ Ⓓ	33	Ⓐ Ⓑ Ⓒ Ⓓ
14	Ⓕ Ⓖ Ⓗ Ⓙ	34	Ⓕ Ⓖ Ⓗ Ⓙ
15	Ⓐ Ⓑ Ⓒ Ⓓ	35	Ⓐ Ⓑ Ⓒ Ⓓ
16	Ⓕ Ⓖ Ⓗ Ⓙ	36	Ⓕ Ⓖ Ⓗ Ⓙ
17	Ⓐ Ⓑ Ⓒ Ⓓ	37	Ⓐ Ⓑ Ⓒ Ⓓ
18	Ⓕ Ⓖ Ⓗ Ⓙ	38	Ⓕ Ⓖ Ⓗ Ⓙ
19	Ⓐ Ⓑ Ⓒ Ⓓ	39	Ⓐ Ⓑ Ⓒ Ⓓ
20	Ⓕ Ⓖ Ⓗ Ⓙ	40	Ⓕ Ⓖ Ⓗ Ⓙ

Answer Key

Pages 8–9
1. D
2. F
3. H
4. A
5. G
6. B
7. C
8. E
9. B
10. F
11. D
12. F
13. B
14. F
15. B

Page 10
1. pre; Sample sentence: We saw a preview of this movie at the theater.
2. un; Sample sentence: The class was unhappy when the field trip was cancelled.
3. be; Sample sentence: We should never belittle someone because he or she is different than us.
4. co; Sample sentence: My mom's coworkers had a birthday party for her.
5. dis; Sample sentence: She had a great distrust of strangers.
6. re; Sample sentence: We will replay the game when the rain stops.

Page 11
1. D
2. F

Page 12
Group 1
B. A child has entered a contest to determine which person has the best reasons for eating a particular brand of cereal.
Group 2
A. He feels that his behaving like a monkey and acting a bit flaky should make him the winner.

Page 13 Mini-Test
1. B
2. J
3. C
4. J
5. A
6. G
7. A

Pages 15–16
1. Tim
2. Sara
3. Abdul
4. Valerie
5. Abdul
6. Valerie
7. Tim
8. Sara
9. Sara
10. Valerie

Pages 17–18
1. Minnie the Mole
2. Minnie's cozy burrow under Mr. Smith's garden
3. the tunnels raised roofs there
4. was placing a trap by her burrow
5. move quickly and follow her
6. two hours
7. Minnie and her children reached Uncle Marty's burrow
8. beavers
9. mole machine

Page 19 Mini-Test
1. B
2. G
3. A
4. H
5. B

Page 21
1. D
2. F
3. B
4. Students' answers should accurately summarize the information in the paragraph.

Page 22
1. fiction
2. a problem
3. the mother
4. *Mom to the Rescue*

Page 23
1. 1994; It allowed listeners to hear sounds almost at the moment they were said.
2. after
3. Eisenhower sets up an agency for technology.
4. A computer network is planned.
5. 8
6. 50 million

Page 24
1. D
2. J
3. D
4. F

Page 25
1. D
2. F
3. Students may note that the author suggests the Yeti may be an "amazing creature," or that "explorers should definitely try to learn more" about the Yeti.

Page 26
1. A
2. J
3. In this version, Goldilocks is taken away to the police station.

Pages 27–28
1. D
2. G
3. B
4. Students' answers should include supporting facts from the passage.

Page 29 Mini-Test
1. B
2. H
3. C

Page 31
1. C
2. F
3. D
4. H

Page 32
1. O
2. F
3. F
4. O
5. F
6. F
7. O

Page 33
1. B
2. J
3. B

Page 34
1. It is a Native American legend about the creation of the Sun and the Moon.
2. It is a Native American legend about the number of months of winter.
3. Both are Native American legends dealing with natural phenomena.

Page 35
Tragedy Answers will vary but may include: about a serious subject; deal with how people treat each; end is always sad
Comedy Answers will vary but may include: expresses feelings of joy; character may surprise others with true identity; good wins over evil
Melodrama Answers will vary but may include: tells story of good against evil; evil villain tries to destroy good characters; problems are solved in end

Page 36 Mini-Test
1. D
2. F
3. C
4. G

Pages 39–42 Final Reading Test
1. D
2. G
3. D
4. F
5. C
6. H
7. A
8. H
9. B
10. H
11. C
12. G
13. B
14. F
15. C
16. G
17. C
18. J
19. C
20. F
21. A
22. G
23. C
24. F

Page 45
1. Students should describe a job they could do in the neighborhood.
2. Students should describe why neighbors would choose them to do the job they chose.
3. Students should describe how they would advertise to get work in the neighborhood.

Page 46
Students' paragraphs should provide detailed, step-by-step explanations of how to complete their chosen tasks.

Page 47
Students' paragraphs should provide detailed accounts of their chosen incidents.

Page 48
Students' paragraphs should provide detailed descriptions of their favorite activities, and should use words that express their personal feelings toward those activities.

Page 49
1. A
2. G
3. C
4. G
5. Students' sentences should be appropriate closing statements for the paragraph.

Page 50
1. D
2. J
3. A
4. H
5. A

Page 51 Mini-Test
1. A
2. G
3. D
4. J

Pages 53–54
1. D
2. H
3. D
4. H
5. C
6. J
7. C
8. tree's
9. Beth's
10. squirrel's
11. cat's
12. brother's
13. fish's
14. sun's
15. bus's
16. door's
17. Jennifer, did you know that your Venus flytrap is eating a fly?
18. I think, Teresa, that we should take my flytrap to the class picnic.
19. Tony, why does your science project include next year's calendar and all those mirrors?
20. To tell you the truth, Joe, I'm trying to find a way to see into the future.
21. Is the electric whatzit machine I made running, Rebecca?

Page 55
1. ad/di/tion
2. an/oth/er
3. cir/cus
4. cloth/ing
5. cou/ple
6. dec/o/rate
7. de/stroy
8. dou/ble
9. fin/ger
10. hap/pen
11. height
12. ledge

Page 56
1. men
2. halves
3. teeth
4. feet
5. flies
6. D
7. F
8. C
9. G
10. A
11. F
12. B
13. J
14. C

Page 57
1. D
2. F
3. D
4. G
5. C
6. J
7. C
8. G
9. B
10. J

Page 58
1. dinosaurs
2. stones
3. ranches
4. yards
5. feet
6. thermometers
7. walruses
8. sandwiches
9. men
10. zebras
11. glasses
12. Germans
13. ostriches
14. helicopters
15. crowns
16. refrigerators
17. turtles
18. teeth
19. pitchers
20. axes
21. children
22. geese
23. cheeses
24. boys
25. villages
26. brushes
27. thumbs
28. movies
29. libraries
30. cities
31. Students' sentences should correctly use the plural form of "mouse," "mice."

Page 59
1. S
2. F
3. S
4. F
5. F
6. S
7. S
8. S
9. F
10. F
11. S
12. F
13. F
14. S
15. F
16. S
17. B
18. J
19. B

Page 60
1. D
2. H
3. B
4. H
5. B
6. Sample answer: Canada
7. Sample answer: Adam
8. Sample answer: Lake Erie
9. state
10. nouns: Yolanda, sister, school; pronouns: her
11. nouns: Karen, volleyball, friends; pronouns: I, our
12. nouns: father, Uncle Ken, meeting; pronouns: My, their
13. nouns: Toby, dress
14. nouns: Randy, Father, seeds

Page 61
1. red, yellow, her
2. Those, their, spelling
3. This, our, new
4. Both, birthday
5. My, busy
6. playful, frisky
7. these
8. two, that
9. two, one, red
10. My, bright, blue
11. smallest
12. twelve, fourteen, Kit's
13. his, shady, elm
14. badly
15. gently
16. surely
17. happily
18. swiftly
19. early
20. brightly
21. loudly
22. carefully

Page 62

1. in the safe
2. during lunch
3. for you
4. in the closet
5. at the museum
6. with the lowest score
7. on the refrigerator
8. under the couch
9. over the bar, on his second try
10. with the most badges

11–18. Students' answers will vary but should include prepositional phrases appropriate for each sentence.

Page 63

1. C
2. J
3. B
4. Tom wanted to be at the meeting, but he had another appointment.
5. Marielle and Trina go to dance class every Wednesday morning.
6. Hunter is deciding whether to go to Space Camp this summer or fall.
7. The test was very difficult, but I think I did well.
8. Grandma bought the presents and decorations for the party.

Page 64

1. B
2. F
3. C
4. does not
5. could not
6. were not
7. must not
8. did not
9. children's
10. frogs'
11. campers'
12. men's
13. horses'

Page 65

1. she
2. me
3. me
4. she
5. I
6. she
7. he
8. We
9. me
10. us
11. me
12. I
13. her
14. He
15. they

Page 66

1. A
2. G
3. A

Page 67

1. C
2. H
3. B
4. G
5. B
6. H
7. D
8. J

Page 68 Mini-Test

1. B
2. F
3. C
4. G
5. C
6. G
7. C
8. F
9. B
10. J

Page 70

1. C
2. G
3. B
4. J

Page 71

1. D
2. G
3. C
4. J

Page 72 Mini-Test

1. B
2. J
3. C
4. F

Page 74

1. C
2. I can ride faster than you can. Let's race to the stop sign.
3. I'm thirsty. Does anyone have some bottled water?
4. We need to be careful on the bike trail. In-line skaters can appear fast.
5. C
6. I love the playground. It has great swings.
7. When I swing too high, I get sick. Do you?
8. C
9. This ride was fun. Let's do it again tomorrow.

10–13. Students' answers will vary but should correctly rewrite each fragment into a complete sentence.

Page 75
1. in the box
2. at city hall
3. under the bag
4. for the library book
5. to the applause; of the crowd
6. to the girls' volleyball team
7. on the list
8. in the dishwater
9. in half; over the fence
10. to the class; with the best attendance

11–18.
Students' answers will vary but should include prepositional phrases appropriate for each sentence.

Page 76
1. Horses can walk, trot, and gallop.
2. The thoroughbred, standard breed, and quarter horse are all used for pleasure riding.
3. Horses are used for riding, racing, and ranch work.
4. Donkeys, mules, and zebras are all similar to horses.
5. The Morgan horse is known for its beauty, good behavior, and endurance.
6. The quarter horse is used as a riding horse, cattle horse, and polo pony.
7. Draft horses include the Percheron, Shire, and Clydesdale.
8. Light horses are used for riding, racing, and ranch work.

Page 77
1. C
2. G
3. C
4. J

Page 78 Mini-Test
1. D
2. F
3. B
4. G
5. D
6. H
7. C

Page 80
1. B
2. J
3. B
4. G
5. A
6. G
7. C
8. G

Page 81
1. adjective
2. adjective
3. adverb
4. adjective
5. adverb
6. adjective
7. adverb
8. adjective
9. adjective
10. adjective
11. adjective
12. adjective
13. adverb
14. adverb
15. adjective
16. adjective
17. adverb
18. adverb
19. Students' paragraphs should provide detailed descriptions of their favorite places and should include a variety of adjectives and adverbs.

Page 82
1. them
2. them
3. him
4. her
5. it
6. them
7. them
8. her
9. It
10. it
11. us
12. it
13. them
14. his
15. It

Page 83
1. their
2. They're
3. there
4. there; their
5. They're
6. their
7. There
8. their; their
9. They're; their
10. their
11. C
12. G

Page 84

Did you know that bats are mammals? Mother bats nurse baby bats when they are young. When the young bats get to be two or three weeks old, they start to find food for themselves. Has anyone ever told you you're "blind as a bat" when you can't find something? If someone tells you this, you can tell them that bats are not blind. They have good eyes and a good sense of smell. Bats are unusual, however, because they bounce sound waves off objects to help them know where they are. This is called echolocation. If you're lucky, you may see a bat. Bats roost in hollow trees, crevices in rocks, and caves. They come out at twilight or at night to look for food. What do you think a bat's idea of a delicious meal is? Well, most of them feed on insects, but some eat fruit, nectar, and pollen. Very few dine on small animals.

Page 85 Mini-Test

1. D
2. F
3. C
4. F
5. C
6. J
7. B

Page 87

1. B
2. H
3. B
4. H
5. B
6. J
7. C
8. F

Page 88

1. patch
2. pos/si/ble
3. pour
4. re/main
5. roy/al
6. slept
7. ti/tle
8. torch
9. tur/tle
10. un/lock
11. veg/e/ta/ble
12. whole
13. wild
14. is/sue
15. lec/ture
16. sta/ble

Page 89

1. undrinkable
2. reread
3. unhappy
4. speechless
5. unsinkable
6. B
7. H
8. B
9. G
10. C
11. F
12. D
13. H

Page 90

1. C
2. H
3. D
4. J
5. A
6. G
7. D
8. J
9. A
10. G

Page 91

1. It's
2. It's
3. its
4. It's
5. its
6. It's
7. its
8. It's
9. it's
10. Its
11. B
12. G
13. B
14. F
15. D
16. G

Page 92

Let's all get together and help the Junior Red Cross. There are lots of people needing the organization's help right now. They're sponsoring a clothing drive to help people caught in the recent flood. Women's dresses, men's shirts, and children's clothing are especially needed. If you've outgrown any clothing or have clothing you don't use, please bring it in. It'll help brighten someone's day!

Page 93 Mini-Test

1. A
2. J
3. D
4. F
5. C
6. G
7. B
8. J
9. C

Pages 96–99 Final Writing Test

1. B
2. G
3. B
4. G
5. D
6. J
7. C
8. F
9. B
10. G
11. B
12. H
13. D
14. G
15. B
16. H
17. C
18. G
19. B
20. J
21. D
22. F
23. B
24. F
25. A
26. F
27. D
28. J
29. C
30. G
31. A
32. G
33. A
34. J
35. D
36. H

Page 104
1. D
2. F
3. A
4. J
5. B
6. J
7. B

Page 105
1. C
2. H
3. D
4. F

Page 106
1. C
2. H
3. A
4. F
5. D
6. H

Pages 107–108
1. D
2. F
3. B
4. F
5. A
6. F
7. B
8. F
9. B
10. F

Page 109
1. B
2. D
3. E
4. C
5. A
6. A
7. H
8. A
9. H
10. D
11. F
12. A

Pages 110–111
1. D
2. F
3. C
4. J
5. A
6. F
7. C
8. G
9. B
10. H
11. A
12. G
13. C
14. J
15. A
16. H
17. B
18. G

Page 112
1. B
2. F
3. D
4. G
5. A
6. H

Page 113
1. B
2. J
3. A
4. F
5. B
6. J
7. B
8. F

Page 114
1. D
2. F
3. D
4. F
5. C
6. G
7. C
8. J
9. A
10. H

Page 115
1. A
2. J
3. D
4. F
5. B
6. H
7. A
8. H

Page 116
1. C
2. F
3. B
4. G
5. D
6. H
7. A
8. G

Page 117
1. C
2. J
3. D
4. G
5. A
6. J
7. D
8. F

Page 118
1. A
2. F
3. C
4. J
5. C
6. H
7. A
8. H

Page 119
1. A
2. H
3. A
4. J
5. D
6. F

Page 120 Mini-Test
1. A
2. G
3. D
4. F
5. B
6. G
7. C

Page 122
1. A
2. H
3. D
4. J
5. D
6. H
7. D
8. G

Page 123
1. 9
2. 8
3. 6
4. 2
5. 6
6. 0
7. 4
8. 7
9. 2
    Rome; Maine

Page 124
1. D
2. F
3. C
4. J
5. B
6. J
7. A

Page 125 Mini-Test
1. C
2. G
3. A
4. H
5. D
6. F
7. B
8. F
9. B
10. J

Page 127
1. C
2. G
3. A
4. J
5. B
6. F
7. D
8. H

Page 128
1. B
2. H
3. D
4. J
5. A
6. J
7. B
8. H
9. D

Page 129
1. A
2. F
3. C
4. G
5. C
6. G

Page 130
1. B
2. J
3. C
4. J
5. D

Page 131
1. C
2. J
3. C
4. G
5. D

Page 132
1. D
2. F
3. D
4. H
5. B
6. F
7. C
8. H

Page 133 Mini-Test
1. C
2. F
3. C
4. H
5. D
6. H
7. D
8. J
9. C

Page 135
1. B
2. F
3. A
4. G
5. C
6. F

Page 136
1. A
2. J
3. C
4. F
5. B
6. H
7. D
8. G

Page 137
1. B
2. F
3. C
4. G
5. B
6. J
7. C
8. F

Page 138 Mini-Test
1. A
2. J
3. A
4. J
5. B
6. G
7. D
8. H
9. C
10. J

Page 140
1. B
2. J
3. A
4. F
5. C
6. J

Page 141
1. D
2. F
3. C
4. G
5. A
6. F

Page 142
1. C
2. F
3. A
4. F
5. D
6. G

Page 143 Mini-Test
1. C
2. G
3. D
4. G
5. A
6. J

Page 145
1. D
2. J
3. D
4. F
5. C
6. H

Page 146
1. D
2. H
3. B
4. J
5. A
6. H

Page 147
1. C
2. G
3. D
4. G

Page 148
1. A
2. G
3. D
4. J
5. C
6. G
7. D

Page 149
1. C
2. G
3. C
4. F
5. D
6. H
7. B
8. F

Page 150 Mini-Test
1. A
2. F
3. A
4. F
5. A
6. J
7. C
8. H

Pages 153–157 Final Mathematics Test
1. B
2. F
3. B
4. J
5. B
6. J
7. A
8. H
9. A
10. J
11. B
12. J
13. C
14. F
15. D
16. H
17. A
18. G
19. B
20. F
21. D
22. H
23. D
24. G
25. A
26. F
27. C
28. F
29. B
30. H
31. C
32. J
33. D
34. G
35. D
36. G
37. C
38. F
39. A
40. H